*Guillaume*

# Also by David Ritz

Biographies

*Divided Soul: The Life of Marvin Gaye*
*Faith in Time: The Life of Jimmy Scott*

Autobiographies

*Brother Ray* (cowritten with Ray Charles)
*Inside My Life* (cowritten with Smokey Robinson)
*The Rhythm and the Blues* (cowritten with Jerry Wexler)
*Rage to Survive* (cowritten with Etta James)
*Blues All around Me* (cowritten with B. B. King)
*Guide to Life* (cowritten with Sinbad)
*From These Roots* (cowritten with Aretha Franklin)
*The Brothers* (cowritten with the Neville Brothers)
*Reach* (cowritten with Laili Ali)

Novels

*Search for Happiness*
*The Man Who Brought the Dodgers Back to Brooklyn*
*Dreams*
*Blue Notes under a Green Felt Hat*
*Barbells and Saxophones*
*Family Blood*
*Passion Flowers*
*Take It Off! Take It All Off!*

Lyrics

"Sexual Healing"
"Brothers in the Night"
"Love Is the Light"
"Release Your Love"
"Can You Tell Me Who the Heroes Are?"

# Guillaume
## A Life

Robert Guillaume
*with* David Ritz

*University of Missouri Press*
*Columbia and London*

Library of Congress Cataloging-in-Publication Data

Guillaume, Robert
  Guillaume : a life / Robert Guillaume with David Ritz.
    p. cm.
  Filmography: p.
  ISBN 978-0-8262-2161-2
    1. Guillaume, Robert.   2. Actors—United States—Biography.   I. Ritz, David.
II. Title.
  PN2287.G795 A3 2002
792'.028"092—dc21
[B]

                                                                    2002074226

Typefaces: Adobe Caslon and LTZapfino

*For Donna*

# Contents

# Preface

I've never collaborated with anyone as candid as Guillaume—not Ray Charles, not Etta James, not even the astoundingly candid Marvin Gaye. Guillaume's candor is straight up. Some celebrities see candor as a means to shock or impress. Guillaume's candor comes out of a desire for self-understanding. He speaks the truth to learn the truth. He approaches self-examination with tough-minded tenacity. When Guillaume starts fooling himself, he's the first to bust himself, the first to tell you. He never backs off from self-confrontation, no matter how delicate or indicting the issues.

Guillaume's great gift is detachment. He holds himself—and the events of his remarkable life—at arm's length. Most stars regale you with self-aggrandizing war stories. Guillaume goes the other way. He presumes you know the good stuff. As an autobiographer, he's looking for the real stuff, the hidden stuff, the stuff that, when it was happening, was too hot to process. In the cool light of day, in the time we take to reflect upon his life, he's eager to process it all. As he describes his gutsy career—his aspirations to sing opera, his steely determination to make it on Broadway, his unexpected triumph on network television—he's far more interested in the ironies than the successes.

I encounter Guillaume some ten months after he's suffered a stroke. I like him immediately. He's an enormously affable man. He walks with a cane, and his speech is slightly slurred. His mind is quick and his banter stimulating. He voices concern about the impact of the stroke on his career. As a lifelong stutterer, I'm eager to compare speech impediments. Turns out that Guillaume and I take the same tack: Get the words out as best you can. If you're talking to a group and the words won't flow, let the group wait. Take your time. Guillaume's approach to time is calming. He never rushes conversations. In our discussions he never skips over events or ideas. Time is a friend, not a foe.

Most of our talking is done in the den of his home in Encino, California. We travel together to St. Louis, Missouri, where he grew up, and explore the geography of his childhood. Over the course of my research, I speak with dozens of family members, friends, and colleagues. As a researcher into his own life, Guillaume is as curious as I am. He presumes nothing. Old ideas—on religion, sex, family, politics, race, theater, television, music—are all up for scrutiny. His close colleagues tell me that the stroke has reduced his physical and intellectual energy. I can only imagine what he was like before. The poststroke Guillaume is full of piss and vinegar. Our discussions are like long-distance verbal jogs, with me huffing and puffing to keep up. As the months tick by, I see his relationship to his stroke as an intriguing combination of acceptance and resistance. Determination is at the core of his character—determination rooted in the realistic.

Guillaume is an intellectual of a peculiar stripe. He's unpretentious and scoffs at being labeled intellectual, but what else to call him? Rigorously educated at Catholic schools, he studied with the Jesuits at St. Louis University and later at Washington University, where he pursued a course in operatic singing. He's well versed in the social sciences and arts. His range of reading is extraordinarily wide, from the heights of Russian drama to the depths of TV comedy. He casts a cold eye on political correctness and says just what he thinks. To hell with voguish ideas.

The joy in coauthoring his book comes from the freedom he affords me. Artistic freedom, a big theme in Guillaume's life, is mine for the asking. "Follow the story wherever it goes," he urges. "Talk to whomever you please. Ask whatever you like." When things get sticky, he never flinches. When I bring evidence of behavior that most men would rather bury, he is ready to reveal. "Let's talk about it," he says. "Let's figure out why I did what I did."

Guillaume is a class act. He has impeccable manners and wonderful social grace. He dresses with quiet flair. As a speaker, he's riveting. He chooses words like a golfer chooses clubs. Guillaume's a straight shooter. He delights in moving directly from point A to point B. At first, I was certain he was square. For much of his life, I believe he was. Conversationally, he can be a fuddy-duddy, proper and sometimes remote. He likes to fence and back you into a corner. But that doesn't last long. Guillaume warms up in a hurry. He's also full of surprises. He professes, for example, to know little about jazz, yet listening to a pianist in St. Louis, he whispers to me, "His style reminds me of Clifford Brown's accompanist, Richie Powell," an esoteric analogy right on the mark. He's incapable of boasting or building up a self-serving case. In discussing the relationships in his life—especially with his sons—he never mentions his acts of kindness and consideration until I ask. He's quick to take responsibility for his negligence, but his virtues must be pointed out by others.

Guillaume is not easy to get to know—and he knows that. You sit with him day after day; you question; you probe; you peel the onion. His mother begins as one kind of person and winds up as another. He presents himself as one kind of grandson but, in the end, sees himself quite differently. As a boy, a man, brother, lover, father, singer, actor, veteran of Broadway and Hollywood, star, stroke patient, narrator of his story, skillful survivor with a vast array of resources, he's both contradictory and compelling. Over and over again, he returns to the basic questions that drive this book: *Who the hell am I? What made me do the things I did?* The forceful integrity behind those questions— and his ability to live with the answers, no matter how brutal—is why I so deeply respect, and even love, Guillaume.

*David Ritz*

# Acknowledgments

David Ritz would like to thank Robert Guillaume, for his unflinching honesty and faith in me; Donna Brown Guillaume, for her invaluable insights and steady encouragement; Eileen Rosaly, John Wesley, Candy Brown Houston, Jack LaZard, Jr., Dolores Maclin, Marlene Williams, Kevin Guillaume, Pat and Odie Carpenter, Roberta Ritz, Alison Ritz, Jessica Ritz, Jerome Samuel Davis, Kandyce Ruffin, Robert Rikki Ruffin, Carla Caldwell, Charzel Davis, Karin Berg, Peter Jason, Phil and Abbie Margo, Alan David, Carol Tillery Banks, Fay Hauser, Marcy DeVeaux, Dan Strone, Reverend Bill Minson, Nicola Goode, Alan Eisenstock, Ben Winters, Mathieu Bitton, Brenda Urban, Aaron Priest, Lisa Vance, Beverly Jarrett, Sara Davis, and Jennifer Brown.

*Guillaume*

# Two Women

I'm a bastard, a Catholic, the son of a prostitute, and a product of the poorest slums of St. Louis.

How did I make it out? How did I get from there to here? How did I get past the confusion of my childhood and find my way in the world?

For much of my childhood, I was told my mother was my sister. I'm not sure when I learned the truth. The role of mother was taken over by my grandmother. She—Jeannette Williams—took over my life. At the same time, I sought the affection of her rival, her own daughter, Zoe Bertha Edwards, my mother. My three siblings—brother James (two years older), sister Cleo (two years younger) and sister Dolores (six years younger)—went by the name Edwards. I was called Robert Williams.

The lies surrounding my mother triggered my anger. But if I was an angry kid, I was also divided: part of me clung to the grandmother who saved my life. That part of me was a goody-goody altar boy who even considered the priesthood until I was told that no bastard could be a priest. Another part of me was an unruly rebel who bucked authority. The two parts clashed. I ran from one side back to the other— sweet obedient child today; in-your-face asshole tomorrow.

I despised poverty. Who doesn't? Poverty fuels anger, even as it fuels the drive to escape. A kind of prison, poverty defines reality and deflates hope.

I was born on November 30, 1927, in the shadow of downtown St. Louis not far from the Mississippi River. The city was still the prosperous rail center of America, but its prosperity did not trickle down. Our tenement was wedged between redbrick industrial buildings and factories that turned out cough drops, paints, balloons, and dry goods. Just around the corner, Lambert Pharmaceuticals manufactured Listerine and the International Shoe Company stitched and soled footwear. I grew up in a world of workers. Only blocks away was the world of imposing public buildings, courthouses, opera houses, fancy hotels, grand boulevards, and ornate movie palaces from which blacks were excluded. The residential sector of our neighborhood, once Jewish, had turned black. Jewish merchants remained prominent but no longer lived by their stores. The movement of money and social status was to the west, away from the levee.

I wasn't conscious of the Great Depression, which hit St. Louis in the thirties. I was too young to understand. I saw the city as an enormous machine humming along at its own pace. We lived in the upstairs back-alley apartment of a two-story row house with neither plumbing nor electricity. We had virtually nothing—cracked linoleum on the floor, dilapidated furniture, a store-bought basin in which to wash, an outhouse in the gravel yard that serviced four apartments and two dozen people. The stench was unrelenting. Our evenings were illuminated by kerosene. We roasted in summer and froze in winter, heat sputtering from a wood-burning potbellied stove.

The emotional heat came from the hostility between my mother and grandmother. It was painful to watch. As an infant, I was in my mother's care. But at age six or seven, I was spirited away by my grandmother. From then on, Jeannette Williams raised me. At that point, Jeannette called her daughter Bunk. I was told that Bunk was my sister. I'm not sure why. Maybe Grandma was protecting me from knowledge she thought would hurt me. Eventually, though, kids learn the truth. The truth, my grandmother told me, was that the scar behind my right ear came from a hot poker wielded by my mother's husband, George Edwards. George Edwards was a powerful man. My grandmother was a powerful protector. As a young woman, my mother had lost her power. She couldn't stop her man from beating me. At least that was Grandma's side of the story. That's why she took me from my mother and left my three siblings behind. *Save Robert; Robert's in danger.* But why Robert and Robert alone?

Maybe because when George Edwards looked at me, he saw proof of my mother's unfaithfulness. Edwards was not my father. My own father had neither a face nor a name. I was never told who he was, what he did, or why he disappeared. Edwards was hell-bent on controlling my mother. My very existence symbolized a breakdown of his control.

I was haunted by other symbols, frightening physical signs of Bunk's violent relationships with men. There were scars on her face, nicks on her hands, cuts on her arms. This in contrast to her stunning beauty, her luminous red-skinned complexion, her dark eyes, and her voluptuous figure. I was also struck by her fine handwriting, a feminine, flowing script indicating a culture that had long been lost. I longed for her love. I might have been an angry kid, but there's not a kid in the world who doesn't hunger for a mother's love.

One moment stands suspended in time:

I was feeling bad. Feeling alone. Feeling like I wanted to be cuddled and held and covered with kisses. That was the moment when I ran to her. By then I knew she was not my sister. I was six years old. She was my mother, and I ran right into her arms. *Shelter me,* I was silently saying; *hold me and tell me it's gonna be alright.*

"*Get away from me, you little black bastard!*" she screamed in my face. I still hear those words.

I got the message. She couldn't stand the sight of me. Didn't want me near her. Didn't want to touch me. Or to be touched. Didn't matter that she was drunk with anger or drunk on booze. All that mattered was the rejection. The rejection hit me like a ton of bricks.

Kids don't understand alcohol. They don't see addiction to it as a disease. I saw my mother's alcoholism through the eyes of my grandmother—as moral weakness. I couldn't see that my mother was sick the way, say, people are sick with diabetes or arthritis. I also couldn't grasp why Bunk was always drawn to worthless sons of bitches.

"Before Daddy," my baby sister Dolores, now sixty-six, recalled, "Mama was a church girl. It was Daddy who put her on the corner."

Dolores's daddy, George Edwards, resembled Adam Clayton Powell, with wavy hair and a high-yellow complexion.

"Daddy was prideful," said Dolores, who devoted her life to professional nursing and the mothering of her thirteen children. "His mother was white, his father was black, and women loved his looks. He had lots of women out there on the corner. He ran rum and card games. One night he was at his game when a man broke into our house. James ran to get Daddy, who rushed home and beat the burglar so brutally that the man had to have a steel plate in his head. Daddy was like that. He'd snap. Another time he heard a policeman talking sweet to Mama. You'd think he'd think twice about striking an officer. Not Daddy. He slapped the policeman silly. And the policeman, knowing Daddy's reputation, did nothing.

"Many were the times he took an open razor to Mama. Bunk would throw up her arms to protect her face, and he'd slash her arms. We'd hide under the bed and muffle our cries, afraid he'd come after us. He made James sit and fan him, like he was a king. He made Mama crazy. Turned her into an angry woman. Turned her mean. She'd leave him, but he'd go after her and drag her back by her hair. He had many women working that corner, but Bunk was his obsession. He made her heel. There was no escaping the man."

Because my grandmother provided an escape for me and me alone, everything changed. Eventually, Grandma brought my three siblings into her home, but for two critical years I was her only child. I felt like she saved me. Jeannette Williams, for better or worse, made me who I am. My feelings for her were huge. I loved her; I feared her; I felt grateful to her; and I was also ashamed of her. She was a servant.

In Grandma's younger days the boys had called her a brick house. When I came to live with her, she was in her early fifties and still had a good body. Her facial features were prominent with high African cheekbones and copper-colored skin. To some she looked like an Indian. I knew she came from Kansas, but that's all I knew. She never mentioned her husband, who had died—or left—before I was born. Like the moon or the sun or the earth beneath my feet, Grandma was simply there.

She was austere. In contrast to Bunk, she was righteous. And rigid. There was nothing second class about Jeannette Williams. She was not the average black woman of her generation, yet she was thoroughly black. She labored all her life as a domestic and took pride in her work. No matter how rich or prominent her employers, which included Catholic clergymen, she was quick to tell them that it was she, not they, who knew how to iron a shirt. She was a professional. She also didn't have attitudes about any particular group. My mother, on the other hand, had all sorts of attitudes.

"Bunk had a thing about dark-skinned colored people," said Dolores. "She didn't like them, and she pushed them away."

I have dark skin, and Bunk pushed me away. Grandma protected me from Bunk's crazy husband, but was she also protecting me from Bunk's antidark attitude? In the war between my mother and grandmother, I sided with Grandma because Grandma had sided with me. I clung to her for dear life. I saw her as saintly. She was God's gift to me, just as I was God's gift to her. If I felt suffocated by her protectiveness, it was a feeling I hid. Acknowledging feelings wasn't part of my upbringing. When feelings came up, I stuffed them back in my head and kept them hidden from my heart.

In the two years that I lived alone with Grandma, I moved between two households. I couldn't stay away from Bunk and my brother and sisters. They were my blood. I couldn't help but be drawn to my mother. She was young and beautiful; she bore mysterious scars. I didn't know she was a prostitute. I didn't know what prostitution was.

These are things I later learned from my sister Dolores, a beautiful chocolate-skinned woman who spoke the quiet truth. I missed Dolores and Cleo and James and often walked across the Eighteenth Street Bridge to Papin Street in South St. Louis, where they lived, in fear, with Bunk.

Fear excites children. Horror movies, for example, break up the boredom of everyday life. George Edwards was a monster in a horror movie. On Papin Street, he and his cronies would be drinking and gambling in one room, my siblings and I would be in another. The voices of the men would be loud, now laughing, now cursing, now boasting or threatening violence. I felt the excitement and the fear. I also felt resentment and exclusion from my siblings, whether real or imagined. In my absence, they had formed an alliance. I was no longer a member of their club. I had been taken by my grandmother; they had been left behind, and none of us really knew what it meant. Was I the lucky one? Or were they lucky for having each other?

"Daddy died when we were still young," said Dolores. "Mama wouldn't attend his funeral. That's how much she hated the man. After that, Grandma came and got us—me, James, and Cleo. We went to live with her and Robert. Bunk came, too, but Bunk was always disappearing. She'd say, 'Kids, I'm just going out for a little while.' We'd beg her not to; we knew that meant she'd be gone for a long, long time. 'I promise I'll be right back,' she'd say. 'You won't be right back,' we'd cry. 'You never come right back.' And sure enough, weeks, sometimes even months, passed before we saw her again. Then one day we'd get home from school and there was Bunk, sober as a church mouse, cooking our meal, washing and ironing our clothes like nothing had ever happened."

Because I cherished my siblings' company, I was happy our family reunited. But I was also pissed that my status as the only child—the chosen one—was demolished. I'd felt privileged living alone with Grandma. Or, as Dolores put it, "Grandma turned Robert into a spoiled brat." Grandma saved her pennies to dress me in a Little

Lord Fauntleroy suit, causing kids to call me a sissy. Like it or not, our family of two became a family of six. Jeannette was the authority figure, the steady provider. Bunk was the bad daughter, the negligent mother, the false sister, here today, gone tomorrow, wild as the wind. Wild also were the fights between mother and daughter, wild and fierce and ugly.

"Reverend DeLoach was one of Mama's boyfriends," said Dolores. "But Grandma liked him too. That's one of the reasons they fell out. They had words over the man. It was sad to see."

Romantic rivalry was another source of tension. Their arguments were hateful. I identified with Grandma. It was Bunk who called me a black bastard, Bunk who lived the forbidden life that threatened our well-being. Yet it was Bunk whose lovely singing voice still echoes in my ear, Bunk whose beauty drew me to her just as her nastiness pushed me away. I remember her dancing with her boyfriend Booby the pool shark, a short man with kind eyes and a quick smile. When they did the two-step in our tiny flat, he'd put his head under her breasts, and she'd place her hands on his head, and they'd dance without a care in the world.

I know things now I didn't know then. For instance, Bunk was only seventeen when James was born and nineteen when I was born. There was a son before James—Lexter. Lexter was born when Bunk was a mere child, fourteen or fifteen. I don't know why it took me a lifetime to finally hear the story of Lexter. Maybe it's peculiar to my family that painful stories were suppressed. Maybe it's typical of black families in this period of American history. I can't say. It's ironic that this story—and others to follow—deepens my empathy for my mother some two decades after her death.

"Lexter would go to sleep standing up," said Dolores. "Mama was giving him a bath. She didn't know he was sleeping, and somehow he slipped from her grasp and fell to the floor. The fall crushed his tiny skull. He died instantly. Lexter was barely one year old. After that, Grandma didn't trust Bunk. She blamed Bunk for Lexter's death.

From then on, Grandma and Bunk would be at each other's throats for as long as they both lived."

The trauma was devastating. I can see why Bunk sought escape through powerful men and strong drink. I can see why her judgmental mother became a constant reminder of her own flaws. I can see why she'd run away from this family—run away from us—only to be drawn back by a sense of love and responsibility, only to be reminded that this was the family she had failed, the family she had to flee, the family that, despite everything, she could never completely abandon. Bunk's story concluded on a surprising high note. But that comes later. For now, I'm still a kid, uptight and confused, living in my grandmother's house in the slums of St. Louis as the Great Depression grinds on.

# Bedrock of My Rebellion

My duality—the good Robert versus the bad Robert, the dutiful grandson versus the defiant renegade—was only intensified by Catholicism. By converting to that religion and entrusting me to the nuns and priests, Grandma exerted her greatest influence. Like it or not, I was to have a strict Catholic education.

For poor blacks, the Catholic Church represented a measure of distinction. I liked that. In no other aspect of life did I feel special or privileged. I got caught up in the pageantry and music. I discovered a talent and distinguished myself by singing church music. That music was born of another culture, but I adopted it all the same. In my mind, the music carried me from the St. Louis ghetto to the magnificent cathedrals of Germany, Italy, and France. At the same time, I resisted the church's rules and regulations. Some of the teachers were prejudiced. Some encouraged me, but others shunned me because of my dark skin.

The church school, St. Nicholas's Elementary, was at 1918 Lucas while we lived at 1916. The church itself was on the corner. Grandma worked at the rectory, where she meticulously washed and ironed the priests' shirts and the nuns' habits for eight dollars a week. Never was a single complaint lodged against her. In contrast, complaints against me were unending.

In the black community, a good education was hard to come by. Grandma saw I had a brain and wanted it developed. The best school in our neighborhood was Catholic. It was the only private school available to us. Credit Jeannette Williams for putting four kids through parochial school. The tuition wasn't exorbitant—this was a *black* Catholic school, and I'm certain fees were adjusted accordingly —but paying for anything beyond food, shelter, and clothing was an enormous burden. Grandma met the challenge. Without a word of complaint, she redoubled her efforts, worked weekends, and found homes to clean as far away as the rich suburb of Clayton. She dreamt of a day when I would rise above my station and find my place in higher segments of society. Her drive became my drive; I absorbed her energy. I wanted to achieve and make her proud. But I also didn't want anyone telling me what to do.

Jeannette Williams understood that education was the key. She believed in rigorous moral and academic training. To her, the church was always right. And the right place to raise kids. She felt especially justified when, over the course of my education, the Catholic diocese in St. Louis became increasingly liberal on issues regarding race. At the same time, racism was rampant at St. Nick's. The white priests and nuns who taught there considered the school the bottom of the barrel. If you were an instructor interested in excelling in Catholic education, you avoided the black ghetto. We later learned that many of our teachers received their assignments as punishment. One nun said that she felt like she'd been sent to Siberia. A priest involved in a hushed-up scandal had been castigated and then sent down to us.

The church itself remained open largely because of its accessibility to downtown. Caucasian white-collar workers found it a convenient sanctuary for confession. And though the discipline of Roman Catholic instruction meant that our training was never slack, we knew both our facilities and faculty were the lowest ranking in the diocese.

I experienced two types of racism at St. Nick's. The first was the racism that any black born in the twenties encountered in any section in the country—whites claiming and legislating their perceived superiority. Such treatment would enrage anyone, but I found a way to deal with it. Even at an early age, I had the wisdom to detach. Color prejudice, the second category, was tougher; it hit me between the eyes. Color prejudice came from both camps—black and white— and, as Dolores said, even from my own mother. Because I felt it so

strongly at a religious school, I grew angry. The terms were clear—
the lighter your skin, the better your treatment. I felt in my gut how
the teachers were repelled by dark skin. Light kids sat up front, darks
in the back. Light kids were called on more readily, darks discouraged
from saying a goddamn word.

I internalized those attitudes. I silently concluded that dark skin
was ugly, a hindrance to social acceptance, and a heavy burden to
bear. A suffering man-God in the form of Jesus Christ was a suit-
able symbol of my own unexpressed pain. When emotion was expressed, its form was pure rage. So I'd pop off, talk back, and drive
the priests crazy. "This boy," Grandma was continually told, "is out
of control."

On the other hand, look at me up there singing with the choir. My
robe is neatly ironed, my hands pressed together in obedient humility.
My voice soars above the others. I savor the attention. I sing solos.
I sing "Ave Maria" with such passion a nun swears I was called to
glorify God. I love pleasing the nuns with my voice. I love learning
Gregorian chant. I learn Latin. Study my catechism. Attend Mass.
Go to confession. Yet give my teachers holy hell.

Why? Why with the passage of time did I develop into a boy, then
a teenager, then a young man so bent on telling everyone to go to hell?
The reasons were mysterious. The good nuns gave us hope, stressing
our potential for achievement and accomplishment. They let us know
that determination could take us far. The strict nuns rapped our hands
with the flat side of a ruler; it was rare to see a nun employ the ruler's
sharp edge. Yet Sister Mary Austin hit me so hard on one occasion
that the imprint of her hand remained visible on my face for weeks.
She was enraged because she felt that I'd humiliated her in front of the
class. Early on, I became an expert at such provocations. No one could
stop me. Some nuns, though, understood me. Sister Claire Joseph,
an inspired teacher, saw my potential and cheered me on. She seemed
to be without prejudice.

The priest who ran the school, though, didn't like anyone darker
than a paper bag. There were rumors of priests messing with the

girls. I saw nothing but tended to believe the rumors. I was told by one priest to "go with the boys and leave the girls alone." He meant that homosexuality was a safer bet than risking pregnancy. But having said that, he let me be and never made a move. One horny nun had no reservations about rubbing the legs of boys who stood beside her desk. Generally, however, nuns were kinder than priests. In facing the priests, I was facing male authority. That was another problem.

Being fatherless, I didn't have a clue about the parameters of male behavior. All I knew was that Grandma enforced the law. The law according to Jeannette Williams said a black boy couldn't exhibit a smart mouth. The priests and nuns agreed. Society not only forbade it, society whipped your ass for it. My grandmother, the daughter of slaves, had been born in the nineteenth century, only a decade or so after the Emancipation Proclamation. She was a survivor and a realist who knew my big mouth meant big trouble. My attitude triggered her worst fears about the ways the white world treated black men. Maybe that's why her reaction to my bad-boy behavior was so fierce. I don't like giving the most dramatic example of Grandma's discipline; it goes against my image of her as savior and saint. But I can't get it out of my mind:

In usual fashion, I mouthed off to one of the priests. I shook his composure and undermined his authority. He got pissed, I got pissed, and I got sent home with the old complaint: Robert Williams lacks self-control. This time, though, the punishment was stiff—suspension for two weeks. Grandma was infuriated. She didn't want to hear my side. According to her, I didn't have a side. She swore this time I'd learn my lesson. Our tiny backyard with its funky outhouse was contiguous with the school playground. At recess, when all the kids could see into our yard, Grandma tied a rope around my neck, then she led me up and down like a pet while my schoolmates mocked me. This went on for two straight weeks. Out there in the yard, tethered to my grandmother, hearing the kids taunt me, I prayed for the ground to open up and swallow me whole. I've never felt so humiliated.

I see now what I didn't see then—Grandma's attempt to protect me from a society whose response to black male insubordination was murderous. Black mothers and grandmothers, especially those without husbands, feared for the lives of their sons and grandsons. But fear can cripple. That's why I'm glad my grandmother's lesson didn't sink in. If Grandma was able to take the teeth out of my anger, it was only temporary. My anger stayed strong and lingered long. Was I angry that I had no father, that my mother was a shadowy figure who pushed me away, or that my grandmother ruled the roost so absolutely? Sometimes I think I was angry because I hated wearing shoes so cheaply glued that even a drop of moisture falling on them meant taking quick steps to keep the soles from flopping and making me look the fool. Maybe I was angry because, even compared to other black families, we never had a goddamn thing. Or maybe I wasn't as angry as I think I was.

"Robert was an extremely friendly and popular kid," remembered Jack LaZard, a handsome dark-skinned schoolmate who became my lifelong friend. "Robert might have been churned up on the inside, but on the outside he seemed normal. He was full of mischief—we both were—but we excelled academically. Robert was also a little star. He had a great voice and won the lead roles in the musicals put on at school. In one such production he sang a song—"Just a Kid Named Joe"—that brought down the house. Well, on one particular night at show-time Robert was nowhere to be found. The show couldn't go on without him. Where the hell was he? I finally found him in a classroom arguing with the nuns who were in his face demanding that, in no uncertain terms, he perform. No one defied the sisters, but Robert was different. Robert didn't budge."

My throat was sore. I'd been yelling and playing ball all afternoon. I could still sing, but the sound of my voice didn't please me aesthetically, so I refused. Was I stubborn? Maybe. Self-centered certainly, self-absorbed absolutely, but when it came to my voice I maintained a cool objectivity. In a few years, I'd realize I had something—natural instinct, wide range, power. I had grand designs to sing opera. Hell, I wanted to the first black tenor at the Met. But I was also a realist, and a survivor, like Grandma. She taught me that you do the best with what you've got.

Jeannette Williams had other wisdom. Despite her close proximity to the world of nineteenth-century slavery, her views on race superceded her apprehension for my safety. She taught not through language, but through behavior. In watching her interact with whites, I saw that she never ass-kissed anyone. Never lost her dignity. When employers were wrong, she told them so. She may have been fearful for me, but she was not a fearful person. The white world of money and power didn't intimidate her. Fate had not been kind. She had to single-handedly support four kids by scrubbing floors and toilets. Yet she was not bitter. If Grandma was frustrated, she transformed anger into discipline. A model of dogged strength, she went to work day after day, week after week, year after year. I never saw her lie, cheat, or steal; and if I committed any of those sins, she'd make sure I couldn't sit for a week.

In the St. Louis of my childhood, racial prejudice was subtle. Southern attitudes prevailed, yet St. Louis wasn't a southern city. It was schizophrenic. Restaurants, movie theaters, and nightclubs were strictly segregated, but public conveyances were not. Neither were water fountains. The presence of two great institutions of higher learning—St. Louis and Washington Universities—did much to liberalize the city. But liberalism could be confusing.

My grandmother cleaned the home of a liberal man named Mel Cronshaw, a designer at the International Shoe Company. As a young kid, I'd go to his home with Grandma on Saturdays. Mr. and Mrs. Cronshaw knew how hard Grandma worked and saw how much my education meant to her. They took an interest in my schooling and treated me kindly. I was impressed with their furnishings and flattered by their attention. I took it to heart. When Christmas came around, I had an idea. Christmas was always a sad occasion for me. Because there was no money, my usual gifts were a chunk of cheese and a work shirt from welfare. Seeing the beautifully decorated tree that the Cronshaws set before their roaring fireplace, I imagined the gaiety of the holiday in their home. These people couldn't have been nicer to me, so I thought nothing of telling Mr. Cronshaw that I could spend Christmas day with him and his family. I had caught him by surprise. He hemmed and hawed before saying they'd be out of town. I took him at his word. As usual, our Christmas was gloomy. But a few weeks later when I returned to the Cronshaws' with Grandma, I overheard Mrs. Cronshaw tell a friend what a marvelous Christmas they had enjoyed—*at home*. My innocence was extreme but understandable. I hadn't known that it was one thing to have blacks in your home as servants, but another to invite them as guests. I'd crossed an invisible boundary and indirectly been told to step back. That hurt. Another incident hurt even more:

My school chums and I would hang around St. Nick's on weekends hoping to make some pocket money from the steady stream of whites attending mass and giving confession. We were street urchins to those parishioners, who, to us, symbolized privilege. We cleaned the windshields and wiped dust from their cars, hoping that proximity to the church would excite their generosity. Across the street was the Black and White Cab Company, a name that fit the traffic around St. Nick's. My brother, James, and I set up a shoeshine box next to the cab stand where white men congregated, waiting for a ride. We were shining the shoes of two such men—my brother and I popping the rag and working the brush—when one of the guys hauled off and spit on my brother's hand. It was no inadvertent act; it was meant to say, *"Take that, nigger."* The glob of saliva oozed down my brother's skin. James and I looked at each other out of the corners of our eyes. I read my brother's expression, and he read mine. We wanted to kill him; we wanted to kick him in the balls. But we were kids, and he was an adult; we were black, and he was white; we were weak, and he was strong. We let reason rule and did nothing. We stuffed our feelings. James wiped the spittle from his hand and went back to shining.

Every Fourth of July we faced similar stuff. We were taught the holiday celebrated independence. Fine. But why did the American Legionnaires have to pile into fire trucks and roar through our neighborhood, dumping bags of garbage and throwing rotten fruit at our homes? Maybe the legionnaires thought it was funny. I thought it was hateful.

Yet I never felt hatred for white people as a group. For all my rebelliousness, I had some positive encounters with white teachers. My grandmother taught me not to judge by color. She saw people as people, not racial representatives. Early on, I realized attitudes of victimization only perpetuate victimization. As I grew older, I heard theories of conspiracy—the white man is plotting our extinction; the white man is obsessed with our annihilation—that seemed farfetched and self-defeating. If such notions were true, only armed rebellion would save us, yet even a kid could see they had the arms while we had shit. Armed rebellion meant suicide. I also knew that if the tables were turned—if blacks were the majority—I'd probably be acting the way whites acted toward me. I'd probably discriminate and feel superior. The more I understood money, the more I saw money as the moving force behind discrimination. Threatened by our willingness to work for wages less than their own, poor whites grew afraid. The older I became, the more I saw racism stirred by ignorance. I embraced my grandmother's wisdom that, by and large, people of reasonable education have reasonable attitudes. It's usually the uneducated who live in darkness and fear.

But even if I was developing tools of detachment, I still felt ugly. I felt dark skin was ugly. And adopting an attitude rooted in the bloody soil of American history, I felt that black was ugly. That was the plain message—from Mama, from the nuns and priests. I was never taught anything else. From elementary school through college, I never heard a word about black culture. I had no sense of the history or accomplishments of my own people. When one's past is invisible, pride comes late, if at all. Slavery was never discussed. All we learned of the motherland came through Hollywood and its ludicrous Tarzan movies in which a white man conquered the jungle while Africans shivered with fear. Other than sports figures, the only black men who made the news were criminals. Joe Louis, of course, was a hero. We danced in the streets when he won and suffered when he lost. Later Sugar Ray Robinson and Jackie Robinson were equally bright stars. But in the classroom, in that all-important arena where official culture is dispensed, black culture didn't exist. There was only the mention of George Washington Carver and his peanut products, hardly inspiring stuff for kids in the concrete ghetto. It wasn't that we were ashamed of our origins; we just didn't know we had any.

I think about the bluesmen who made a name for themselves when I was growing up—Arthur "Big Boy" Crudup, Sam "Lightnin'" Hopkins, Muddy Waters. Later they were worshipped by white musicians and placed in the canon of American popular culture. But in the thirties and forties, we were told their music was vulgar and without value. True music—God's music—was European and white, not African and black. My grandmother adopted this attitude, and I'm afraid I did too. I felt the sensuous swing of Basie and Ellington, but I also felt drawn to what teachers insisted was high culture.

In other cultural areas, I resisted the party line. A big part of St. Louis public life was the Parade of the Veiled Prophet, a yearly ritual during which high society rolls through the center of the city. To mark the start of the season, an extravagant procession with flowers and floats and maids of honor snakes its way down Washington Avenue. On the central float is the prophet himself, concealed beneath a veil and sequined robes. I never understood the veil, but I sure as hell understood the role of blacks in the parade. The only black participants walked behind the floats and cleaned up the horseshit. When the pageant wound its way through our neighborhood, the black kids took peashooters and hid behind a billboard. Our response to the pageantry was to pelt the Veiled Prophet. The more we hit our mark, the happier we became. Maybe it was only kid's stuff, maybe it didn't have social significance, but I *was* conscious of being poor, and I *was* conscious that the Veiled Prophet was rich, and I did feel defiant. How else could I express my contempt for a society that so blatantly excluded me? The parade made it clear: the abundance was not to be shared.

I am grateful, though, to have shared time with a man who made a singular impression upon me. We called him Uncle Jack. Because Grandma was gone until early evening—especially when she worked in the suburbs—she had Uncle Jack sit with me until she came home. He fascinated me. Jack was an itinerant farmer who sold rubbery vegetables up and down the streets. I still see him seated at our kitchen table, his skin glowing in the light cast by the kerosene lamp. He loved to play solitaire. He'd slap down one card and snap up another. While he played, he whistled the blues. I mean, the man could whistle. And he would sing. His blues were hypnotic. His voice was filled with feeling. He moaned low:

> Got the key to the highway and I'm bound to go
> Say, I got the key to the highway and I'm bound to go
> Gonna leave here runnin' cause walkin' is most too slow.

# Morning Glories
# and Pigs' Snouts

When I was still a young kid, we moved to Nineteenth and Franklin, the central corner of my childhood, the corner I thought I'd never escape. Seems like I stayed on that corner forever. It was the worst part of the central east end, miles from the Ville, the black middle-class neighborhood to the north. We lived off a back alley in rooms that were dismal and dark. The only sign of hope was Grandma's flowers. She grew morning glories and azaleas in window boxes. I'd monitor their growth, waiting for that spring day when the blossoms would open. I loved those moments. I loved how my grandmother saw beauty in seeds and soil and blooming vegetation.

I didn't love my grandmother's work ethic, but I knew not to fight it. I wouldn't have had a chance. No matter my mood or circumstance, I worked. I worked at whatever job I could find. Before I was old enough to comb the want ads, I hawked newspapers in front of the International Shoe Company as thousands of workers streamed out in early evening. "Get your *Star!*" I screamed. "Get your *Democrat!* Get your *Post-Dispatch!*" The news grabbed me—Germany on the move, Prohibition repealed, John Dillinger murdered, the Lindbergh baby kidnapped, Roosevelt reelected, the Hindenburg exploding over New Jersey. I stood there hollering the headlines, realizing that the world was big and St. Louis small. I was excited to envision a world outside my own where heroes and villains vied for power, where wars were fought and governments toppled. Part of me hungered to wander that world, but another part was afraid. All I had, all I knew, was St. Louis—and the steady support of my grandmother.

Yet I did manage to wander. I went off to Kansas City. I found the courage when I was a teenager. Summer had arrived. By then I was an expert at scanning the want ads. The key was the word *boy*. All ads that didn't include that word were to be ignored; all ads that did, circled. Errand boy, water boy, paperboy, delivery boy, shoeshine boy— at one time or another I did it all. Slowly I grew conscious of how, by studying these ads, I was looking straight down the barrel of discrimination. You didn't need to be a linguist to know "boy" meant black. "Boy" also meant substandard pay. "But some pay," said Grandma, "is better than no pay." When I finally found an ad that promised $1.35 an hour—practically a fortune—I was elated. It also meant that my buddies and I would have to take the train across the state to a spot some ten miles outside Kansas City, where the Missouri Pacific was hiring young men to lay track.

We set off with high expectations. We were no longer children; this was men's work. We reached the campsite at high noon under a blazing June sky. We were ready to go to work and make that good money. We were shocked at what we found: big, beefy, ugly guys— some weighing three hundred pounds—stretched across their bunks as they slobbered and sucked on pigs' snouts. Flies swarmed everywhere. In the corner of the tent an enormous woman, her face beaded with sweat, stood over a boiling pot. Did we want a snout? No, thank you. As we saw the size and weight of the iron tools we'd have to haul, as the brawny workers belched and farted, we knew what we had to do—get the hell out. We were scared. And because we were also broke, we had to walk back home, 254 miles to St. Louis. Sleeping by the side of the road, eating berries and fruits from trees, we made it back in seven exhausting days. Suddenly the ads for delivery boys sounded good.

In the days before faxes and e-mail, delivery boys had a big role. I worked for Dun and Bradstreet, a position with some prestige; the documents I carried often revealed a company's net worth. I liked sneaking a peek at the figures. I didn't know what the numbers meant, but I knew they were substantial. I wanted substance. I still sought that measure of distinction.

Because Catholicism offered such a distinction, I didn't abandon its rites and rituals until I was in my thirties. My ego required that distinction. And even though my wiseass ways got me thrown out of St. Nick's several times, I graduated and went to St. Joseph's School for the Colored, a private Catholic institution for grades nine through twelve. Like St. Nick's, St. Joe's engaged priests and nuns who, due to miscues somewhere in their careers, were forced to instruct blacks. Some had racist attitudes; others didn't. The disciplined structure and traditional course work served me well. I excelled academically. But that didn't stop the screw-you side of me from bucking authority. And, believe me, St. Joe's had no shortage of authority figures to buck.

Sister Anna Adelaide was the principal, also known as the warden, a tough old bird who, without a second's hesitation, threw open the door to the boys' bathroom, marched in, and apprehended the crap-shooters crouched on the floor. That other boys were pissing didn't bother her in the least. I spent hours in her office. Once, for instance, I was defending my brother, who was blessed, unlike me, with an even temperament. We were in the same classroom when he was falsely accused of talking. Because he was reluctant to respond, I spoke up for him. "But I'm not talking to you," said the nun. "But I am talking to *you*," I said. I was thrown out of school for a week. At home, Grandma hammered me with the same message as my teachers and, for that matter, society did—*no loud-mouthed black boy will amount to much.*

In spite of these endless battles, I enjoyed some recognition for the solos I sang with the choir of St. Anne's Church. The church was next to the school and distinguished by its Romanesque architecture, its facade wrought in the gray-white limestone typical of St. Louis. An ornate church has special pull for the poor. All the shortcomings of our own residence—lousy heat, nasty outhouse, lack of electricity—stood in marked contrast to the amenities available at St. Joe's and

St. Anne's. Going to church meant indoor plumbing and lots of light. We were broke, but at least our religion was rich. It provided a place where we could go to the bathroom and not freeze our asses off.

On the streets, some of our non-Catholic friends took us to task and called us sissies. Ironically, that antagonistic attitude fed our sense of exclusivity. At the same time, I sure as hell wasn't about to be excluded from our neighborhood gang. In the thirties and forties, the word *gang* was less ominous than today. Knives were ubiquitous, but I hardly ever saw a gun. The gangs weren't much more than a silly excuse for a bunch of street urchins to guard the 'hood. The Counts and the Rats were to the south, the Termites to the west. We—the Nineteenth Street Aces—protected our five-block province. *Do not trample our turf.* I'm surprised I had the balls to join up. I never ranked high in the pecking order. Couldn't even consider myself a sword carrier since I never owned a knife. I just went along for the ride. The minute Grandma suspected my involvement, I quit the Aces. I was far more afraid of Jeannette Williams than any street gang.

"It was our sister Cleo," my sister Dolores remembered, "who protected us from the really rough gangs. Cleo was a light-skinned beauty who could and frequently did pass for white. All the boys wanted her. In those days it was all about color. She was a star of the neighborhood. Even though Robert was two years older than Cleo, she had more street smarts. I remember when Robert was at the Marquette movie theater where gang-bangers were threatening him. They wouldn't let him leave. When Cleo heard about it, she ran over. Soon as she showed up, the boys backed off. They let Robert pass. Cleo made sure no one touched her big brother. She had that kind of power. The hoodlums were in awe of Cleo. They'd do anything for her."

Cleo wore her hair like Lana Turner. She knew how to apply makeup; she knew how to dress. She became a glamour queen. For awhile she went with the Greek owner of the Lincoln Café, a popular neighborhood spot. He'd take her to upscale nightclubs—Tune Town, for example—from which blacks were excluded. Cleo's beauty gave her access to a world we couldn't enter. Ultimately, that world proved deadly. In the jargon of the day, my sister lived a viper's life, the same life led by our mother. Cleo's story finally turned tragic—doubly so because no one was sweeter or wittier. It broke my heart to see her fall. Before that fall, though, Cleo was there for me. She helped me weave my way through the neighborhood. Cleo clued me in—this guy is cool, that guy isn't; go here, avoid going there; don't cross this dude, trust that one. Cleo didn't seem to resent those two years when I lived alone with Grandma. She helped me through uncertain times and insulated me from danger.

Meanwhile, I traveled the unsteady road that leads from adolescence to adulthood. Grandma steadied me and my siblings as best she could. She fed and clothed us without fail. If we were confused and frightened by our mother's comings and goings, Grandma was as dependable as the rising sun. And though she ruled with severity, there was a warmth to her household—a sense of well-being—that soothed. She poured her love for her grandchildren into her meals: the panfried chicken, the cornmealed buffalo fish, the biscuits and syrup and hot molasses and butter, the sweet sustenance that kept our stomachs filled and our bodies strong.

At school I stayed with the music. European history permeated every part of my vocal education. From the devotional strains of "Ave Maria" to the medieval harmonies of Gregorian chant, I was attuned to another continent, another culture, another time. In my own culture, I was aware of the controversy surrounding contralto Marian Anderson. In 1939, the Daughters of the American Revolution barred her from singing in Constitution Hall in Washington, D.C. It was only through the intervention of Secretary of the Interior Harold Ickes that she performed on Easter morn before seventy-five thousand spectators at the Lincoln Memorial. Because she was black and

talented, I was inspired. Her male counterpart—Roland Hayes—
loomed even larger in my imagination, not just because he was black,
but because, like me, he was a tenor. Later I'd emulate his style and
adopt his repertoire. Anderson and Hayes sang the occasional Negro
spiritual, but the heart of their repertoire was European—German
lieder, French art songs, Italian arias. Despite the significance of their
role as pioneering black artists, Anderson and Hayes looked to the
Old World, not the New, for the bulk of their musical material.

When I was a teen, the only New World music came in the form of
the drum-and-bugle corps I joined at school. (I didn't know it then,
but even that form sprang from Germanic roots.) We played the usual
John Philip Sousa fare: "Semper Fidelis" and "Stars and Stripes Forever." I played drums, and James blew the bugle. We were good. In a
city filled with crack units, ours stood out. We never executed fancy
stepping and twirling horn techniques; our style was staid and highly
traditional. But St. Joe's was serious enough about the corps to re-
cruit two top jazz musicians—drummer Cecil Scott and trumpeter
Howard Gant—to tighten our beats and sharpen our licks. We did
well enough to go to Chicago for a contest, where we placed second.
With its towering skyscrapers and high-flying energy, Chicago impressed me. I'd never seen a metropolis seething with such ambition.
In contrast, St. Louis was fast asleep.

Football was St. Joe's other field of competition. I was a spectator,
not a player, although most of the players were not much heavier than
me—115 or 120 pounds. We played the white Catholic high schools,
whose teams had bigger players and better equipment. We were humiliated. Our guys had no spikes, just regular street shoes; our uni-
forms were secondhand rags, while our opponents wore brand-new
jerseys. Our boys were malnourished compared to the brutes across
the scrimmage line. We got slaughtered. We tended to discount the
disparity in size and nutrition; we were sure we'd win anyway. And
every now and then when we fielded someone with the speed to
dart into the end zone for a touchdown, we screamed as though

Jesse Owens himself had made the score. Such moments, though, were rare.

Going to football games, marching in the band, singing in the choir of St. Anne's, attending high masses, confession, and Holy Communion, pursuing young women who caught my eye—it all came to a boil just when the world was fighting a war that was finally going America's way. Just as I was thrilled when Joe Louis beat Primo Carnera, then James Braddock, and, finally, Max Schmeling, I was rooting for our guys to beat back the Germans. Patriotism was part of our schooling, and, despite my rebelliousness, I was patriotic. This, after all, was the forties, a time when I rooted for our Cardinals baseball team, lily-white as they were. When the Brooklyn Dodgers were in town, though, I and every other black citizen of St. Louis cheered for Jackie Robinson to smack the ball out of the park.

There's also the matter of my sex drive. It was strong. All my life I've desired women, sought them, courted them, and, after sex, kept my distance or simply disappeared. It began early. I lost my virginity when I was fifteen. I can't remember her name. Her face was pretty and her body developed. That's all that mattered. We were in her home, and her parents were out. It happened on the couch. It was over before it began. I couldn't call it satisfying. Neither of us had any idea what we were doing. We went through the motions. I bragged to my friends; I exaggerated how long it lasted; I elaborated on its pleasures. I told myself that, finally, I was a man.

My sex drive operated as a silent submarine, accelerating so smoothly I wasn't even aware of its strength. I had a steady girlfriend at sixteen, but that made no difference. I was randy. Within a few weeks my girlfriend had caught me with someone else. Secret assignations were too exciting to pass up. That set the pattern for much of my life. In the fifties, when I found a lady with whom I enjoyed a free and far-ranging physical relationship, I realized how restricted my experience had been. Until then, the act was perfunctory. I didn't get the subtleties. In my teens and early twenties, it was enough to meet a girl whose face and figure stiffened my resolve. I was all about lust. And impatience. I wasn't crude or overbearing in my pursuits, but I was tenacious. I worked hard to get laid. Ironically, my easiest conquest was a Catholic girl who, upon completion of her novena—nine days of devotion to the Virgin Mary—blessed me with the gift of sweet surrender.

Meanwhile, I was still regimented by the conventions of church, state, and domesticity. I still believed in heaven and hell; I still believed all non-Catholics were doomed. But the single issue that separated me from doctrine involved masturbation. I couldn't stop. After all, I had firsthand evidence of its pleasures. Still, the church considered it sin. But sin or not, my practice continued for longer than I'd like to admit.

I grew increasingly hostile at St. Joe's. My fresh mouth worked overtime. When an acerbic remark of mine infuriated a priest, I was kicked out on my ear. This was nothing new. It was my senior year, and all I had to do was cool my heels a couple of weeks before going back and graduating. But this time was different. This time I decided to turn my world upside down and get out for good. This time I said fuck it.

# "Boy,
## One of Us Has to Go . . ."

War stirs the psyches of young men like nothing else, despite the human loss associated with it. The high drama of World War II diverted the attention of blacks living in the ghettos of America's big cities. Whatever feelings I had about racial inequality at home, I never doubted the rightness of America's position abroad. America was fighting for freedom. Implicitly, that meant my own freedom, a position that, if naive today, made sense when the world was aflame.

The army had strong selling points: I could earn considerable money, and my expenses would be paid. I could instantly enlist in a great adventure; I could escape St. Louis and a home where grandmother and mother were still at war; and I was promised big veterans' benefits. I could always return to school. My timing was good. The war ended in the summer of 1945; I didn't turn eighteen until that November. By the time I reached Okinawa the action was over. I was determined to stick it out, get my coin, reap the benefits of the G.I. Bill, and call it a day.

Once overseas, I tried to defuse my temperament to suit the military setting. Tried, but didn't succeed. From time to time, I'd lose it. Once I lost it playing craps. Back home I'd learned to lock the dice six and one, prattle them back and forth to avoid tumbling, and increase the chances of making my point. A black soldier accused me of foul play. He bad-mouthed me until I smacked him upside his head with a straight left shot. He was too surprised to retaliate, and I prevailed.

I didn't prevail, however, in my efforts to go along and get along in the army. I'm from Missouri; my white captain was from Texas; I had no sense that I was obliged to make him feel comfortable. It wasn't in my nature—just as it wasn't in my grandmother's nature—to act obsequiously. When he insinuated his superiority, I made it clear that I didn't feel inferior to anyone. Of all the manifestations of racism, the one that infuriates me most is the presumption that color equals stupidity. I could never let my superior officer feel superior.

He couldn't stand that, despite our differences in color and rank, I viewed him as a peer. I'm sure he saw me as uppity. The fact that I spoke correctly and employed a decent vocabulary riled him. What I had been taught in school—that correct bearing would enhance my progress—was backfiring. This man found my demeanor insupportable. If I had been mature, wiser about the ways of the world, I would have avoided him. I should have stayed out of his way and denied him the satisfaction of putting me down. By baiting him—or allowing him to bait me—I was playing into his hands. When he called me into his office, I didn't know what to expect. His southern accent was thick as molasses.

"Boy," he began, employing the single word he hoped would kill my composure, "this Army ain't big enough for the both of us. One of us gon' have to go. And Williams, which one you suppose that's gon' be?"

"Would that be me, sir?" I asked, unruffled.

"You got that right, boy. Here's how it's gon' work: You ain't gon' be eligible for induction, reinduction, enlistment, or reenlistment."

*So far, so good,* I thought. I didn't care if I never saw the army again.

"Something like this," he warned, "can follow you for the rest of your days."

*I ain't important enough for anything to follow me for the rest of my days,* I thought.

"But what I will do for you, boy," he went on, "is avoid an dishonorable discharge."

"Thank you, sir," I said, realizing that, despite this man's antipathy, I was getting everything I wanted—getting out and getting my benefits to boot.

Just like that, after eighteen months of frustration, I was being excused for nothing more than an insupportable attitude. I would later learn an aphorism that perfectly describes the situation—*what is grace in a white man is arrogance in a black man.*

I returned to St. Louis and my grandmother's place at Nineteenth Street and Franklin Avenue free of distinction or disgrace. My main accomplishment was retaining elibility for G.I. Bill benefits, which meant a free college education. But that also meant completing high school. Reenrollment at St. Joseph's was not appealing. I procrastinated, putting my education on hold as I worked at the post office. I secured a position as a classified sub and was on my way to becoming a regular postal clerk. In the forties, the job was considered a plum for a young black man, but civil service was not my speed. I also found work as a packer for a dry goods firm in the wholesale district. My supervisor was unrelentingly critical, watching my every move. Finally, adopting the attitude my grandmother conveyed when she was told how to wash shirts, I told the man, "If you want to pack while I supervise, I'll be happy to do so. But if not, leave me alone." Mercifully, he left me alone.

My guilt about leaving school, however, did not leave me alone. One afternoon after work I was at St. Joe's fraternizing with old friends when Sister Anna Adelaide took me aside. Even though she had once expelled me, she'd always believed in me. "If you'd like to return," she said with obvious sincerity, "I'll arrange it. You'll always regret not graduating high school." Despite the fact that I was bringing home money, my grandmother made the same argument. I had to agree. I reenrolled at St. Joseph's, maintaining my post office job and matriculating at the same time. By the spring of 1947, I'd managed to satisfy my course requirements, avoid ejection, and was set to graduate.

Graduation coincided with a turning point in the history of the city. Newly appointed Archbishop Joseph Ritter was, unlike his predecessor, a liberal. (Rumor had it that the previous archbishop, John J. Glennon, had instructed his servants in the chancellery to smash all dishes off which blacks had eaten.) In 1947, Archbishop Ritter ordered the integration of the city's Catholic schools. His policy affected over two hundred elementary and secondary schools. The South Siders were up in arms, but the archbishop meant business. He did not mince words; his meaning was clear: *Cross me on this, and you will be excommunicated.* They got the message.

For the first time ever, the graduating class of St. Joseph's would receive diplomas together with the classes from white Catholic high schools at the Cathedral Basilica on Lindell Boulevard. The cathedral is adorned with the largest collection of mosaics of any single building in the world. It stands as an awesome monument to the power, wealth, and art of Catholicism in St. Louis. I was excited to be graduated in the great sanctuary—and doubly excited to be part of the archbishop's pioneering plan for integration.

Several days before graduation, we were to report to the Cathedral Basilica for rehearsal. We, the black seniors, were instructed by the nuns to wear ties, white shirts, and dark pants and mind our p's and q's. When we arrived at the church, we were startled to see the white students, who outnumbered us dramatically, sprawled on the cathedral's limestone steps, chatting. Some were smoking cigarettes; others were making time with their girlfriends; all seemed relaxed beyond reason, casually attired, and acting like they were at a picnic. While the white kids lolled about, we were admonished to stand erect and silently parade inside single file like soldiers. I resented the double standard. Why were only they allowed to relax? Why were they and they alone permitted to have fun and act normally? We were told that it was our responsibility to reflect well on our race—a line of reasoning I'd hear often. I don't remember the actual graduation. But that rehearsal burns in my memory, that day when the white kids had a ball while we marched into church like zombies, fearful that someone might think we were actually human.

For the next decade, I remained in place, torn by a slightly different version of the same duality: I wanted to leave; I was reluctant to leave. For the next decade, St. Louis would contain me, reassure me, infuriate me, bore me, lull me into a waking sleep, fill me with false dreams, excite me with intriguing possibilities, educate me, alienate me.

By now my grandmother was in her late sixties, and a lifetime of arduous labor was evident in every aching step she took. The long flight of stairs that led to our place on Franklin became insurmountable. "As Grandma got older," Dolores recalled, "she didn't want to go out. She'd worked herself to the bone, and her energy was gone. In 1947, she also had a slight stroke. But it wasn't the stroke that kept her from going down those stairs. Physically, she was still capable of getting around. Emotionally, though, she wasn't right. Fear had set in. Grandma withdrew from the world and became reclusive."

I, too, withdrew at the very point in my grandmother's life when she needed me most. I found a room in a boardinghouse and moved away from Nineteenth and Franklin. I couldn't deal with my grandmother's incapacitation. I remember being in church as a young boy when Grandma arrived for Holy Communion. She didn't know I was there, but I watched her every move. Walking down the aisle, she suddenly stumbled and fell—maybe because she was spent from working all day, or perhaps she was feverish. Either way, I did nothing. A Polish woman helped her to her feet. All the while, I hid in the shadows, ashamed. In my mind I feared that this black woman, unsteady and unstylish, would bring shame to our family, shame to me. For all she had done for me, I couldn't accept her. My ambivalence toward Jeannette Williams was torturously deep. And as I witnessed her decline, I lacked the character and moral fiber to lend support. I had the nagging feeling that she expected—and, God knows, deserved—her grandchildren to ease her burden. This grandchild, though, for all she had meant to him, was emotionally unavailable.

Another grandchild, Cleo, had also fled. I wanted to convince her to stay but lacked the ethical authority. "Cleo went off with Jack to Chicago," Dolores recounted. "Jack was her pimp. None of us wanted her to go, but Cleo was headstrong. She liked pretty things, and knew how to get them. She knew how to play men." As the family philosopher, I was expected to say something, to show Cleo the error of her ways, to point out that she was following the disastrous pattern of our mother. What *could* I say, though? We remained dirt poor. I was working as a low-level postal clerk. James was off in the navy. Dolores was still in high school. After a lifetime of honest work, Grandma was on the verge of physical and mental collapse. Is this what Cleo had to look forward to? How could I argue for good old-fashioned values? Where was the evidence that diligent labor paid off? Cleo was offered the easier route. She was stunning. She had style. She wanted the feel of silk and cashmere against her skin; she wanted to wear fancy hats and lacy dresses, ride in luxurious automobiles, go to glamorous places, date exciting men. Men fell over themselves for her favors and promised her the moon. This man Jack said, "Come to Chicago. We'll grow rich together. We'll live in style." I said nothing. My heart was heavy, my head empty of arguments.

"She wrote me soon after she got to Chicago," said Dolores, "and sent money for my graduation dress. I got to buy the dress of my dreams. A little later, she sent me a bus ticket to visit her. Chicago was everything I had imagined. Cleo and Jack were living in a lovely house. Her closet was filled with clothes. We drove around the city in Jack's big Cadillac and I thought everything was all right. Then one day I was alone in the house when a white man came to the door looking for Cleo. 'She's not here,' I said. The man looked me over and said, 'You'll do.' 'I'll do *what*?' I asked, knowing full well the answer. I ran out of there and caught the first bus back to St. Louis."

The same viper's life that had lured my mother lured my sister. Cleo didn't know—none of us did—that the life promising comfort would only bring misery. Later, the two women—Cleo and Bunk—would exchange roles in a twist of redemptive irony. But that was decades away. Meanwhile, as Cleo's life spun in one direction, mine spun in another, toward the center of the city. I headed for St. Louis University. Where was my head? I was considering college. And the fact that St. Louis University was Catholic and dominated by Jesuits had particular appeal. The Jesuits elevated learning to a high intellectual level.

I saw them as protectors of the faith. I liked how their theological arguments were grounded in cold logic. I fell under their sway and began viewing myself as a logician, deriving satisfaction from the definition of logic that, some fifty years later, still resonates: logic, I was taught, is that systematic body of scientifically established rules and principals essential to straight, clear thinking. Straight, clear thinking is what I pursued, and straight, clear thinking is precisely what the Jesuits served up for breakfast, lunch, and dinner.

I did well in philosophy. My teacher liked my papers on Aristotelian logic and encouraged me to write more, hinting that, with dedication, I might have a career in academia. I fancied myself a junior philosopher. I devoured Shakespeare, and where other students groped for the meaning, the text seemed clear to me. I might have stumbled over the rhythms of iambic pentameter, but I clearly divined the import of "neither a borrower or lender be." I argued with my English professor over interpretations of Spenser's *The Faerie Queene* and, in doing so, thought I was hot stuff. The prof disagreed. He gave me a "C" in the course. Only years later did I realize the ridiculously pompous figure I was cutting in class. I was unable to control my mouth; my arrogance was still on full display.

I read *Paradise Lost* intoxicated by its allegorical passion. John Milton's world made sense; his Satan seemed a living, breathing character, not an abstract notion of evil but a flesh-and-blood demon whose pain and anger I could feel. I related to his fury; I understood how his psychological makeup had him rule in Hell rather than serve in Heaven. In describing the primacy of God and man's fall from grace, Milton fired my imagination, forcing me to reflect upon myself. Was I falling or rising? What was my own state of grace?

I couldn't claim much. I carried heavy shame. I started associating with other St. Louis University students. At times I felt their intellectual equal; mostly, though, I felt inadequate. I worried that if I grew too close to them, they'd discover where I lived. And where I lived was not a good address. Underneath, I still harbored anger about being so poor, but I blamed neither my family nor society for my lack of fortune. I simply was who I was. Out of the army, out of high school, attending college on the G.I. Bill, a twenty-one-year-old guy looking to get laid, looking to find in the ivory tower what I'd had never found in real life—an answer, a system to cling to. I desperately needed to succeed at something.

Despite my concern with philosophical morality, my own morals were questionable. I pondered these issues in the abstract; applying them to my personal life was something else. Truth be told, that life had its shady element. For awhile, I associated with poolroom players who were out-and-out criminals. They were stealing checks out of mailboxes, cashing them, and using the money to buy clothes at Wolf's Men's Store. I was envious. I craved fine clothes myself. I recall, for instance, my first pair of good pants, or as we called them, drapes. They were a blue herringbone, pleated, tapered, and cuffed so that they broke sweetly over the top of my Stacy Adams lace-ups. Like a fool, I wore the drapes during a touch football game, where I fell and tore the fabric at the knee. I considered suicide. I would have killed for a hundred-dollar worsted wool suit by Hart, Schaffner and Marx. I wanted fancy straws and fine Stetson fedoras. I wanted to wear the best, not only for the satisfaction that goes with everyday narcissism, but because I saw how women responded. Cats with cool threads got cool chicks. But I was never a cool cat. Never hip. Hipness also involved flaunting the rules. My raw fear of the police kept me from illegal activities. I stopped short of crossing that moral boundary. Principle didn't stop me; fear did.

I see now that I did cross moral boundaries in respect to women. My consciousness in the forties—hell, my consciousness well into the eighties—was nil. On psychoemotional matters concerning male-female relationships, this male was comatose. The pattern I followed could be boiled down to a single crude phrase—*find 'em, fuck 'em, and forget 'em.* I looked hard at women, hoping one might look back at me. When she did, when she liked what she saw or was moved by what she heard, I moved in quickly, and, after the deed was done, might or might not reappear, depending upon the lady and the circumstances of the courtship. Later in life, it was suggested that my interactions with women mirrored my mother's interaction with me—*here today, gone tomorrow.* I'm no apostle of Dr. Freud's and have avoided the analyst's couch. It'd be foolish, however, to discount the obvious: mothers imprint patterns of behavior upon children that last a lifetime. Couple that with my ambivalence toward my grandmother, who was more of a mother than my mother herself, and it becomes clear why I became a hit-and-run man. If a woman was too good (like Jeannette Williams), I might feel tied to her forever, unable to realize my own freedom; if a woman was too bad (like Bunk), I might avoid involvement for fear of being dumped.

I offer no excuses. The facts are these: In 1950, I fathered a girl named Patricia. Her mother, Mary, was a delectable beauty whose sister married my brother, James. They were daughters of a preacher. When Mary became pregnant, I was perplexed. Marriage was neither considered nor discussed. Our brief affair was hardly memorable. As best I recall, Mary made no demands. I walked away from the relationship, from both mother and daughter. If I experienced guilt or regret about abandoning a girlfriend and child, those feelings were suppressed. Almost by osmosis, I absorbed an attitude common to black men of my generation. The attitude, born out of slavery, was, *screw all you like and damn the consequences.* The more you copulated, the happier your slave master, the greater his work force and profits. Since slaves were not only non-Christian but subhuman, Christian morality was put on hold. Again, I'm not offering excuses but just explaining the cultural ethos influencing descendants of both slave master and slave. That isn't to say I'm not responsible for my every action. I surely am. But, at the same time, my personal history—all our personal histories—are linked to a greater American history that must have an impact on our thoughts and actions.

Any way you look at it, I was on the prowl. So it makes sense that I would have opened a dress shop. What better way to meet women? But there was another angle. Despite encouragement from professors, I lacked the patience for scholarly pursuits. I sought excitement, and I wanted money. I wanted to be an entrepreneur. If I was so smart, why couldn't I figure out a way to get rich, or at least be comfortable? But it was something I couldn't do alone. I knew I needed a partner with the experience and confidence to tackle free enterprise. Why not Jack LaZard, my companion all the way from St. Nick's to St. Joe's? A supersharp guy, Jack had won a full scholarship to St. Louis University and also had experience in retail. What Jack really had, though, was the guts to take on the system and start something of his own. I sought to emulate his spirit.

"I had worked for merchants in the city ever since I was kid," Jack recalled, "and the pattern was always the same. I'd start out sweeping the floors, then selling, then even buying merchandise from vendors, and finally learning every part of the business. Merchants told me how impressed they were with my ability, but I'd still wind up in the shipping room. I could be running the whole operation, yet never get the advancement or, most importantly, the money. One man even said it to my face: 'You're good at this, boy, but certain positions are not open to you people.' That's when I knew I'd have to make my own opening."

Opening our own business was fun. There were three of us—Jack, John Hightower, and myself. Our first ready-to-wear shop was downtown in the People's Finance Building, where many black professionals had offices. Our mistake was in not securing ground-floor space. Business was slow. Our second location was better, right on Franklin between Nineteenth and Twentieth, my old stomping ground. Our theory was that if we sold at least one pair of hosiery to every woman we knew, we'd make it. Our theory failed. Ultimately the business failed. We were undercapitalized and underinformed about the vicissitudes of retail. But for a year or two, we squeezed by.

Charzel Davis was a schoolmate at St. Joseph's, a close friend, and a customer who remembers the Geraldine Shoppe, named after Hightower's sister. "The store was lovely," said Charzel. "The first thing you noticed was the floral wallpaper in red and pink and white. The wallpaper complimented those floral-patterned dresses so popular in the forties. Jack and Robert were standing there behind the counter, clean-cut young men who looked enough alike to be brothers. In those days it was especially impressive to see young brothers take this kind of initiative and own anything of their own. They carried quality merchandise, comparable to the skirts and blouses you found at the better department stores. They had a flair for fashion. It also didn't hurt that Robert was handsome and popular. There was something appealing about shopping at a women's store overseen by good-looking young men."

Not appealing enough, I'm afraid, to make a go of it. Geraldine's had a certain élan and, had we profited, the store might have made a merchant out of me. But I lacked focus. Aside from money, I didn't know what I wanted. Free enterprise was an appealing concept on paper, but I wasn't willing to exert the effort. Moreover, we were too inexperienced to compete. When expenses finally overwhelmed revenue, we closed the doors, and I walked away. Jack went on to succeed in other retail endeavors. I went on to work as a dishwasher and a candy cook.

So much for my dignity. So much for my half-baked college education or secret dream of being a singer. As the forties turned into the fifties, I was in my twenties and merely knocking about. Washing dishes in a Chinese restaurant was grunge work, especially with no dishwashing machines. Seemed like five thousand customers a night were wolfing down chop suey and looking to me to scrape their damn plates. Also worked at Red Cross Cough Drops where I cooked syrup to crystallize into candy. My shift went from 4 P.M. to midnight.

Knocking about in St. Louis inevitably meant winding my way to East St. Louis, the anything-goes city that sits just across the Mississippi in Illinois. That's where, as we said back then, I got my ashes hauled. East St. Louis meant gutbucket juke joints, fast action, and sexual intrigue. I was always square, a straightforward guy too mired in convention to break rules. I was uptight. But I wasn't uptight enough to pass up a night with friends in those wild towns beyond East St. Louis like Brooklyn, Illinois, where you'd hear Howlin' Wolf or Muddy Waters or Ike Turner in the days before Tina. This was a world that, though controlled by the white mob, was reserved for blacks. Sprawling steel and coal-processing factories lined the river and marked the landscape, their smokestacks coughing excrement into the sky. But after sunset, the streets of these satellite cities east of civilization gave off another odor. The smell of sweet perfume wafting through a smoke-filled club, the sweat-soaked bodies of big-boned women, everyone rubbing to the rhythms of get-down blues—man, those joints were jumping.

St. Louis had nightlife of its own. We graduated from the neighborhood movie houses—the Marquette, the Roosevelt, the Comet, the Douglass, and the "Funky" London—to the Club Riviera where you'd see royalty: Count Basie, Duke Ellington, King Cole, Earl Hines. I worked up an imitation of Billy Eckstine singing "Cottage for Sale" and "I Apologize." I could approximate Al Hibbler and the Ink Spots, but my Eckstine was stellar. Stars had emerged from St. Louis, and we were aware of the myths surrounding them. Rankled by racism, Josephine Baker escaped to Paris to find international fame. Others, like comedian Redd Foxx, were still carrying on at the Midnight Ramble, the revue following the Saturday night movie at the Regal. On one of our evenings out, friends might take me to an after-hours spot where I'd find myself sitting across from Dorothy Dandridge. She was absolutely gorgeous, and I was overwhelmed to be in her presence. But if my cronies gushed over her, I didn't. I detached; I felt apart. Or maybe I just had a *need* to feel apart. Maybe I was posing. Maybe I was full of it. Either way, this business of detachment remained a strong part of me. I saw it like this: If I gush over Dorothy, and she rejects me, I'm crushed. I maintained that same attitude when I got into show business. Feign indifference long enough and grow a tougher skin. As an emotional tool, it both served and injured me—keeping me from a nervous breakdown, but also keeping me from my real feelings.

There was a moment, however, when real feelings emerged. I had no choice. Even though I remained in a never-never land of lost dreams and unfulfilled ambition, even though I did my best to skirt all entanglements, this turn of events stopped me in my tracks. I don't think I've ever recovered. I still deal with it daily, haunted by sensations of grief, guilt, and self-contempt. I'm speaking of the death of my grandmother.

# Jeannette Williams
# (1880–1951)

In my mind's eye, I see a monument to my grandmother in my backyard. Perhaps it's of classical design, a bronze bust of her face revealing her high African cheekbones and penetrating eyes. Or perhaps it's rendered by a modern sculptor who, commenting on the tedium of her life, depicts her bent over a mop and pail. I fantasize about such tributes because, in fact, there are none. No grave, no tombstone, not a single marker. The best I can do is offer this book as testament to my confused love and gratitude surrounding this wonderful, powerful, controlling woman.

She was seventy-one when she died; I was twenty-four. For all my supposed talent and intelligence, I had accomplished nothing. I had no money. And I had no access to money. Her strength had begun to wane some four or five years before her demise. I could have prepared; I saw it coming. But I had no interest in looking. It was painful to see this robust woman turn sickly and frail. She battled asthma; she contracted pneumonia. And if, as Dolores suggested, her malady was also psychological, that was another reason to stay clear. Mental deterioration was as frightening to me as failing flesh.

When Grandma died in the spring of 1951, I could no longer contain my cool about familial ties. For several years, I had avoided the family. We were all moving in radically different directions. Cleo was turning tricks. James had joined the navy but been falsely accused of stealing and dishonorably discharged. In my view, that single event cast a dark and permanent shadow over him. His spirit broken, he spent the rest of his days working below his capacity, his dreams dashed. Dolores was still a teenager and Jeannette's devoted caretaker, doing for our grandmother what I never could. Bunk exhibited the same qualities that had frightened and angered me ever since I was a child. She appeared and disappeared, sometimes sober, often drunk.

In short, our family was in tatters. The death of Grandma only deepened the divisions. Making matters worse was the financial burden that had never been lifted from Grandma's life. Our only hope was an insurance burial plan into which she'd been putting pennies for years. Even during the depression, when two cents made a difference, she kept up the payments. So when the family congregated at her home, her lifeless body in the bed where she had slept for a half-century, we anxiously opened the envelope marked "Burial Policy." The bottom line was brutal: we could lay claim to a paltry forty-eight dollars.

She had bought a plan that an insurance company could only sell to the poor. There was now nothing to be done. Rather than face the truth and deal with my own inadequacy, I excoriated Bunk for her intolerable behavior toward my grandmother. I was obsessed with giving my mother her comeuppance, and picked a hell of a time to do so. The truth I hid from my heart was that I had not only abandoned my grandmother but couldn't even pay for her funeral. The one thing she wanted—a decent burial—was the one thing I couldn't give her. How I could I be so goddamn ineffectual? What in God's name was wrong with me that I didn't have the resources to pull together a few hundred bucks? It was ridiculous. Inexcusable. I couldn't forgive myself. And still haven't.

When the workers came from the city morgue and carried off her body to be dumped in a common grave, I cried like I've never cried before.

I say now that I was filled with self-loathing, but I wouldn't have used those words in 1951. Rather than explore my feelings, I stuffed them. Decades passed before I understood what the loss of Grandma represented. I couldn't admit that without her the best I would have been was a common criminal. I didn't want to consider what her life and death meant to me. It took forever to acknowledge attitudes earlier suppressed. As ugly as it sounds, part of me was waiting for Grandma to die. Part of me wanted her to die. In some pocket of my imagination, her death meant my freedom. As long as she lived, I was not only emotionally tied to her by apron strings, I was tied to the cycle of poverty from which she never escaped. Her pain was my pain, her poverty my poverty. Jeannette Williams was a symbol of a generation unable to break the chains of a caste system that imprisoned her. I believe that's why, when I came of age, I abandoned her. I was afraid I'd turn out like her—a servant. If she were gone, maybe I could finally feel free as the wind.

None of this means I didn't love the woman. I loved her dearly. But I had a way of avoiding inconvenience. And it was inconvenient in those final years to care for Grandma with the same devotion she had lavished on me. So I slipped away before she died, and I slipped away after she died. I looked for distractions. I returned to life as usual. I continued bouncing from one odd job to another. On most levels I saw myself as a failure. It was only the dream of domestic bliss and a family of my own, a family to replace my troubled family of origin, that pushed me into a new direction. I sought entry into the middle class. To achieve that end, I courted a lovely girl while, at the same time, I became a streetcar driver.

In the early fifties, the Public Service Corporation, the bureau that controlled the streetcars, advertised for drivers. Until then blacks had been barred from sitting behind the wheel. The public nature of the ad, though, resulted in a lawsuit overturning the racist policy. I interviewed for the job, a book of poetry tucked under my arm. I made a good impression and was praised for being well-spoken. "But instead of reading that poetry," said the supervisor, "you better be studying the driving manual." I was hired and became one of the first blacks to drive a streetcar in St. Louis.

I wore a uniform, controlled a massive piece of machinery, and, by passengers both black and white, was viewed as a pioneer. All this appealed to my ego. After the financial catastrophe surrounding Grandma's death, a steady, salaried job calmed my panic. And besides, what other positions were open? It was strangely satisfying to circumnavigate the city with such prescribed direction. My route took me from Olive to Franklin, the cornerstone of my youth, all the way up Delmar. The fun of maneuvering the enormous car tickled the little boy inside me. Heading west from downtown, I drove with a determination to keep the demons of self-doubt at arm's length.

I began viewing women in a different light. After my grandmother died, a certain sobriety crept into my thinking. My old duality—the dutiful Robert versus the defiant Robert—was still there. But with Grandma gone, my rebellious side softened, at least for a minute. I wanted serenity. I sought solace in a sort of idealized lady, someone pretty, petite, demure, and light-skinned. That doesn't say much for my racial-political awareness, but that's where I was at. I was interested in a white-looking black woman because she satisfied my sense of female beauty—and because her appearance afforded me status. It was also important that she be Catholic. I was still attending mass and singing in choirs and conventional enough to resist looking outside Catholicism for a romantic relationship. In 1953, I initiated such a relationship with a stunning eighteen-year-old beauty who fulfilled my ideal. Her name was Marlene Scott.

"When I first met Robert," Marlene recalled, "I was a senior at St. Alphonso's Rock High School. At twenty-six, he was eight years older. My friends thought it odd for me to go with a guy that age, but I was taken by Robert's sophistication and charm. It helped that our first meeting, singing in the choir of St. Malachi's, seemed sanctioned by the church and accompanied by sacred music. It also helped that my stepfather and mother knew the people who owned the boarding house where Robert stayed. They approved of him, but who wouldn't? He was handsome, self-assured, articulate, and extremely kind. In our community, he was seen as a gentleman and, though I knew his people had been poor, we weren't exactly wealthy ourselves.

"When it came to courtship and settling down, Robert was far ahead of me. I was still a child, but he had aspirations of family. Things would have moved much slower were it not for a terrible accident that took the lives of my parents. It happened in 1954. In May, a month before high school graduation, my mother and stepfather were driving over the bridge from East St. Louis. In the midst of a rainstorm, their car skidded and crashed into an iron girder, killing them both. I went into shock. I'd never encountered such loss before. I'd never encountered tragedy of any kind. My mother and I were extremely close. I didn't see how I could live without the comfort of her love and protection. For months after the funeral, I'd look for her in crowds, on buses, among those seated in church. Then she came to me in a dream. 'Mother dear,' I asked, 'when are you coming home?' She looked straight in my eyes and firmly said, *'Baby, I'm not coming home.'* With that, I awoke. The dream helped me. It was her way of saying I'd have to move on. And moving on meant finding another kind of protection and family comfort. I felt Robert offering that sort of comfort, and I was in no position to resist. The death of my parents changed everything about the way I viewed the world. It also changed the way I viewed Robert. Maybe I saw him as my savior."

I saw life slipping away from me. I felt the need to order the chaos in my head. Marlene was a lovely girl with lovely manners, a sweet disposition, a personality not unlike that of the women on TV sitcoms who played amiable adjuncts to their all-knowing husbands. I wanted to live in a sitcom. I wanted normality. At the same time, I grew dissatisfied. A streetcar driver has lots of time for reflection. The weekly check was reassuring, but it didn't hide the symbolism of the work: not only was I riding around in circles going nowhere, I was trapped inside the circles of my life in St. Louis. The route represented a prison of my own making. How to get out?

For years I'd suppressed my ambition to sing professionally. I'm not sure if it was because I feared failure or simply lacked spunk. After Grandma passed, though, I was more willing to seek singing opportunities outside of church. I sang recitals at places like the Pine Street Y, rendering classical pieces or spirituals in a style that lacked refinement. I needed a teacher. I also needed intellectual stimulation. I hadn't been to school since dropping out of St. Louis University three years earlier. College called.

At the same time, my middle-class dreams of a quiet home and a picture-perfect wife were more vivid than ever. If my relationships with women were confusing, what better way to escape the uncertainty than to propose something permanent? I wanted the emotional neatness that comes with well-ordered domesticity, a woman who admired me, a household to head. Because Marlene was so young and dependent upon what should have been my greater wisdom—but clearly was not—she endorsed my false feelings of empowerment. I looked like I was in control; I looked like I knew what I was doing. I even fooled myself.

"Robert and I were married in 1955 at St. Malachi's," said Marlene, "the same church where we had met in the choir. It was a small wedding, and I remember there was sadness in the air. I was thinking of my mother and how terribly I missed her. Robert might have been thinking of his grandmother. I'm not even certain his own mother attended. I know that deep down he had awful conflicts about his family, but those were issues he never discussed. I never told him this, but I realize it now: If my own family had been alive, if my parents had not been killed, they never would have approved our marriage—not while I was still so young. Mother would have insisted that I wait, reminded me to be cautious, and alerted me to the differences in our ages. Because I was a devoted daughter, I would have honored my mother's wishes. But she was gone, and I was alone. I was lonely and desperate for someone to count on. Robert had the smarts to take on the world. He was mature, and also talented. I admired his voice and knew he could sing his way into greater things for us all. I married a man with ambition enough for the two of us."

My maturity was a facade. In truth, I was as lost as ever, divided between a desire for uncomplicated domestic bliss and the need to excel. Ironically, at the very moment I wanted to break out, I fenced myself in. There was no woman sweeter than Marlene, and no man more deluded into thinking that such sweetness could contain his confusion. It wasn't a marriage of passion but of appeasement. In three short years, even as Marlene gave birth to our two precious sons, the marriage sustained damage from which it never recovered.

The turning point was my decision to return to college. This took me into a world that excluded Marlene and excited me in ways I hadn't anticipated. Because I had already attended St. Louis University, Washington University held fresh appeal. The G.I. Bill allowed me to take courses free of charge. And the university, one of the best in the country, had a reputation for liberalism and, most important, included the Blewett School of Music, which offered a wide spectrum of practical instruction.

In the Eisenhower era of 1955, the civil rights movement was just beginning. That year, after the arrest of Rosa Parks, Martin Luther King joined the bus boycott in Montgomery; in Mississippi, Emmett Till, a fourteen-year-old black boy from Chicago, was brutally murdered for whistling at a white woman. Though those events troubled me deeply, they seemed to transpire in another world. The Washington University campus was a world all its own, an island on the west end of the city, lushly beautiful and distinctively European. Its graceful towers set it apart; its heavily wooded campus, its manicured lawns, its long green vistas and dramatic quadrangle afforded a quiet tranquility. It was a place far less nervous than the noisy streetcar life I led only blocks away. Miraculously, racial tension hardly existed; social mingling of whites and blacks was not uncommon. I cut back my hours on the streetcar and spent more time on campus.

I fell in with a group of wanna-be intellectuals who congregated in the basement of the college Y. My intellectualism was suspect, but I enjoyed bantering with serious-minded students. Among them was Oliver Nelson, who'd soon go to New York to take his place among the great jazz arrangers and composers of the modern era. And among my professors was Leslie Chabay, an Hungarian Jew who had spirited his wife and son out of Budapest in 1936. Escaping Hitler, they rode to Switzerland by bicycle. From there he and his family headed to New York where he performed with the Metropolitan Opera, the ultimate aim of singers such as myself. He had a strong reputation for his *buffo* roles and had recently come from Bennington College in Vermont where he was artist in residence. His duties at Washington included private instruction. I was among his students.

I had a reasonably good voice, which I employed badly. Chabay addressed that faulty employment with patience and practicality. He also introduced me to the wonders of Mozart and Purcell and, though I had some acquaintance with lieder, Chabay's passion for nineteeth-century German art song was contagious; I grew wild for lieder myself. Chabay took a personal interest in me. He invited me join him for lunch at his home, a gracious residence filled with books. Chabay had a genteel spirit and never failed to encourage. I owe him much. But I also owe a woman who was even more instrumental in my professional progress. She was so important to my life that I have invited her to explain how her story intersects mine.

# Karin Berg

"I met Bob at Washington University. We were both outsiders, both alienated from the worlds in which we were raised—mine white, his black. My early life was marked by my parents' alcoholism. They were alienated from their own families, where they were considered black sheep. My origins are Norwegian, Swedish, and Finnish, though my parents' exact lineage is murky. As an only child, I would be left alone when they went off to drink. Only Daddy would come back to check on me. Mother was too bombed to care. When I was twelve, she died of cirrhosis of the liver. I learned much later that Bob and I shared similar backgrounds; we both had alcoholic mothers who were deeply troubled and emotionally unavailable.

"Emotional trouble also came to me in the form of scoliosis. When I was fourteen—this was 1950—I was in a body cast for three months, but the procedure didn't work, and my back remained curved for the rest of my life. In high school, a single pimple is enough to ruin your self-esteem, so you can imagine the effects of scoliosis. There went my dreams of being an actress. My father and I lived in a couple of furnished rooms in South St. Louis where, despite his drinking, he cared for me. He was a staunch Republican, but also a liberal. I adored him and adopted his politics of compassion. I remember the day he told me of the lawsuit that allowed blacks to drive streetcars. 'If you encounter a black driver,' he said, 'be kind and friendly because others will be scornful.' Daddy also took me to the ballpark to see the Brooklyn Dodgers play the Cardinals. When Jackie Robinson came to bat, Daddy said, 'Stand up, Karin. Stand up for a great American.'"

When I met Karin, I was impressed with her knowledge of jazz. She knew the music and also the jazz life. As a teenager, she had hung out at clubs like the Crystal Palace and associated with jazz aficionados and sophisticated songwriters. She told me that when her father died just before she entered Washington University, it was only the joy of listening to jazz—its creative spirit and open sensuousness—that kept her together.

At school, Karin was a rugged individualist. She never moved into a dorm. She took two streetcars to get to Washington. Against all school rules, she insisted on living alone in the furnished rooms where she'd grown up. The dean of women sent her to the dean of men who, seeing her as an oddball, made an exception. Karin loved the liberal bent of the faculty. Washington University had a long list of Nobel Prize winners. McCarthy-inspired witch-hunts were still common, and professors warned us when they suspected government agents were in the classrooms. Karin identified with several teachers—especially those championing the poetry of e.e. cummings —but the student body was another matter. They called Wash U a streetcar college—an apt description in my case and in Karin's— because locals dominated. The town-and-gown synergy was cordial enough, but we never felt part of mainstream campus life. Social structure was weighted in favor of fraternities and sororities and reflected the hierarchy of St. Louis with its grand notion of the Veiled Prophet. It wasn't surprising, then, that I wound up in the campus Y along with the other independents. Among them was Karin.

We were societal refugees. The fact that we hung out in the basement seemed to symbolize our underground status. It was there that Karin started the college jazz club, where she pointed out the glories of Miles Davis, Stan Kenton, and the Hi Lo's. Karin also started writing for *Student Life,* the campus paper, and was full of opinions, whether on the virtues of Adlai Stevenson or the evils of Roy Cohn.

"When I met Bob," Karin remembered, "he hadn't shed his image of the Good Altar Boy. I don't say that facetiously. There was a sweet side to him that offset his sarcasm. The fact that he was older—I was nineteen, he was twenty-eight—removed him from the rest of the group. He was also married while the rest of us were single. On face value, Bob lived like a square, but I saw him as hip. He viewed the world unconventionally; he had daring, challenging points of view; he was brilliant. We were instantly compatible and intrigued by one another. The day we met we went from the basement of the Y to Lee Hall cafeteria, where we had lunch and spoke all afternoon. We discovered that we were each rebelling in different ways. Bob was strikingly good-looking, and I'd be lying not to admit that he knocked my socks off. But our initial bonding was based on ideas, not sex. We simply loved talking to each other. I was having problems with my boyfriend, and Bob became my confidante. I could tell him anything without being judged or belittled. In no time, we established a strong friendship."

For my part, I was tremendously attracted to Karin. Her scoliosis didn't detract from her appeal. She was slight and soft-spoken; her blond hair was long and lustrous; her Scandinavian facial features were delicate; and she was stimulatingly bright. This first friendship with a white woman was exciting. Such social intercourse was only possible on such a liberal college campus. I was amazed that I could relax with someone whose background was so dissimilar and yet close to mine. Of all Karin's alluring qualities, though, it was her essential kindness that drew me to her. Ironically, she had far greater feeling for African American music than I. When it came to jazz and gospel, blues, and rhythm and blues, Karin was downright evangelical. She taught me. In turn, I surprised her with the sort of music I pursued, and, though it was far from her taste, she was strongly supportive.

"The first time I heard Bob sing," she recalled, "I was stunned. He was singing lieder at a campus recital. I didn't know what to expect. I knew nothing about the genre, and then suddenly here's this perfect German enunciation, this powerful tenor voice just resonating with sincerity. I heard an angelic side to Bob I didn't know was there. When he sang, he let down his caustic armor; his soul shone through."

Singing took me places I'd never gone before. It was at Washington University that I met Caralee Coombes, a soprano with whom I sang duets. She invited me to practice at her family home secluded in the white suburbs. We rode the bus together, walked the tree-lined streets of her exclusive neighborhood, and rehearsed in the well-appointed parlor where her mother left us alone. Like Karin, Caralee was far ahead of the racial curve. She lived in the kind of grand house my grandmother used to clean. I took it all in—the white world of comfort and grace—and luxuriated in the engaging music we made together.

At the university, I appeared in "The Saint of Bleecker Street," a modern opera by Gian Carlo Menotti. The setting was the Italian community in New York's Greenwich Village. I had a small part, but when the lead male sang of his alienation from his people, when he bemoaned being misunderstood and accused his compatriots of judging him, my heartbeat quickened. I related. The character's angst spoke directly to me.

I felt apart from the worlds in which I lived—the black world of St. Louis, the white world of Washington University. I had no idea, no real sense of direction. To make up for my uncertainty, I spoke with absolute assurance. I'd argue you down in a hot minute. I had to be right. Yet I tried to be polite. If the majority of my friends saw me as pleasant, that was the image I chose to convey. I needed to be in control, or give the impression of control. Outside, I looked good. Inside, I was a mess.

Marlene gave birth to our first son, Kevin, in 1957. I hadn't told her—she wouldn't learn until years later—that I had a daughter by another woman. Why complicate matters? My heart was happy to have a son, but my heart was also heavy with worry over increased responsibility. As my family expanded, so did my secret desire to escape St. Louis and find fortune elsewhere. When, for example, Chabay got me a scholarship to the Aspen Summer Music Festival, I didn't hesitate. I ran off to Colorado as if my life depended upon it.

I went alone. I justified leaving Marlene and Kevin because the scholarship covered only my expenses. But the truth is that I increasingly saw music and family as competing enterprises. My old duality was reemerging—the dutiful husband and father over here; the renegade artist over there. Aspen was thrilling. I was happy to meet other singers from around the world and even happier to perform in concerts where the standards were high. We'd sit under shady Aspen trees and study those majestic mountains while, from a distant dorm, someone played a recording of Swedish tenor Jussi Björling—our hero—doing Donizetti. The real world seemed far away. Turned out, though, that the real world was as close as Cleveland.

Russell and Rowena Jelliffe caught one of my performances in Aspen and, afterward, introduced themselves as the directors of Karamu, a community center in Cleveland. Though the Jelliffes were white, Karamu was a training ground for black artists. (In Swahili, Karamu means meeting place.) "We're inviting you to join our company," said the Jelliffes. "There are many roles that would suit you. Think it over." I was flabbergasted and, I admit, afraid. Flabbergasted because, in spite of my evolving musical activity, I still doubted my talent; and afraid because I realized Cleveland represented an escape from my family that could prove irresistible. I was torn. "I'm flattered," I told them. "I'll certainly consider your offer."

I did all I could *not* to consider the offer. I knew acceptance would undermine domestic bliss. Still, the offer loomed large. Karamu was highly regarded. When would such an opportunity be offered again? I returned to St. Louis, intoxicated by Aspen and the promise of Karamu. I went back to Marlene and our infant son, back to the streetcar—up Delmar, down Delmar—back to Washington University, where Chabay, told of the Karamu offer, urged me to take it.

Like so many artists, I was caught halfway between high arrogance and low insecurity. Unlike the blues, where there's no formal training, classical music offers a strict academic agenda. If you wanted to be a blues singer, the best you could do was convince Jimmy "Mr. Five by Five" Rushing or Big Joe Turner to take you under his wing. To sing opera, though, you went to college and bought what the universities were peddling. I'd been buying Chabay's program and hoping for the big payoff—a career in opera. I had a three-and-a-half octave range, ample power, but a naturalistic sound that was not operatic. I lacked the tone and texture required for grand opera. I sounded like a loud folksinger. And, to make matters worse, I oversang, a deficiency that took decades to correct. Yet in spite of all this, Chabay saw something. "If you continue to work hard," he urged, "you might have a future in show business."

*Show business?* The words I wanted to hear were, "You'll make it all the way to the Met." I wanted to enter Valhalla, where William Warfield, Roland Hayes, and Paul Robeson ruled. But I was also a streetcar driver being driven crazy by going up Delmar and down Delmar, up and down, down and up, over and again, echoing a play by Sartre: *No Exit.*

College was no longer possible for Karin. She quit her sophomore year. Her teachers were shocked. Her writing for *Student Life* was good enough for one instructor to promise her placement at the *St. Louis Post-Dispatch* once she graduated. She was making A's in her English courses, but she was miserable. She couldn't get over feeling ostracized. She was the ultimate outsider, and even the camaraderie of the indies in the basement of the Y wasn't enough to make her stay. At Washington University, she, like me, always felt "less than" and "not enough." Karin belonged in the jazz world with the beatniks and the hipsters. So she left school and went to work at Union Electric as a typist. Her typing skills saved her. When friends asked Karin what she really wanted to do, though, she'd say, "Run away to New York and become Bette Davis."

Her opportunity came when a girlfriend moved there. She invited Karin and her former boyfriend to come along, and that was it. Later, Karin told me how, emerging from the Lincoln Tunnel and seeing that skyline for the first time, she had wept. The beauty, the possibilities, the energy were overwhelming. I missed her and thought of her often. She wrote that she was finally in a city, unlike St. Louis, where she could buy books by Henry Miller.

"I was passing through the gates of heaven," she said, "only to experience hell for the first eight months. I worked as a typist at Columbia University Teacher's College. I spent all my money on jazz clubs in the Village. I loved seeing Miles and Monk and Charles Mingus, but no city in the world is lonelier than New York. I clung to my ex-boyfriend, but that was little comfort. I took on the big city, yet the big city proved colder than I could have imagined. No matter, I was determined to stick it out. At the same time, when a friend in St. Louis invited me to her wedding, I didn't hesitate to run home— not permanently, but at least for a respite. That's when I ran into Bob, and our worlds suddenly collided."

My duality deepened: I wanted to go to Cleveland; I wanted to remain with my family and be a responsible breadwinner; I wanted to stay at Washington University, quit Washington University, quit driving a streetcar, find other ways to make money, get off my ass, move to New York, and sing at the Met. I was mired in conflict. I left school because I realized that academia was not for me. I lacked the studiousness to pursue a career as a teacher or scholar, and, as far as music goes, I had gotten all the instruction available at Washington University. Chabay came right to the point: "Now it's a matter of putting what you learned to practical use." That meant Karamu, where the scale pay was minimal—far too low to support myself and my family. Besides, Marlene was pregnant with our second child, Jacques, motivating me to stay put and seek ways to make money.

I returned to my old fantasy of becoming an entrepreneur. This time a friend and I were convinced a hair product we'd been selling door-to-door would turn the trick. Among blacks, hair has long been an obsession—especially the transformation from kinky to straight—

so we deduced that a pomade, packaged properly and sold aggressively, would hit big. After finding someone with a formula, I came up with a name—Sassy Curl. We developed two labels, one peddled door-to-door as Sassy Curl; the other, though the identical product, was offered to salons as Sassy Curl with Triton X400. We thought we were marketing geniuses. We put the stuff in small flat jars that resembled the containers for Dixie Peach, the best-selling pomade of the day. All we needed were investors. With five hundred bucks, we'd be off and running.

I was so keen on the scheme I quit my streetcar job, something I'd been aching to do for years. Never wanted to drive up and down Delmar again. All this entrepreneurial energy also cancelled out Cleveland—at least for awhile. At the same time, I had to scramble for temp work. That's how I wound up as a waiter at Peacock Alley, a jazz club. The after-hours ambience threw me in with a rough crowd. I was on the fringes of the hustling life, watching friends roll drunks. On one sad occasion, I went along as a half-assed accomplice. There was something attractive about the predator's style. His swagger was infectious; he didn't give a good goddamn about what you or I thought. Just took what he wanted. In the back of my mind I figured a decent score could finance Sassy Curl. But to witness the rip-off itself, to see some poor tanked-up soul robbed of a few dollars and left without carfare home . . . well, that turned my stomach. I found the deed so foul I never again considered a criminal act.

"I was back in St. Louis for this wedding," Karin remembered, "when one night I went to hear jazz at Peacock Alley. I began descending the staircase that leads to the club when I saw this black man in a waiter's uniform standing at the bottom. His arms were crossed, his head was cocked, and he was staring straight at me. It was Bob!"

Karin and I hadn't spoken to each other in a year, and I was glad to see her. She flew down the stairs and embraced me. "Cool it," I said. "Remember where you are." St. Louis wasn't New York. White women didn't hug black men in public. I asked her to sit quietly as another waiter served her. At the end of the evening, I drove her home, and we talked till four in the morning. At that point, our friendship was still platonic, but I could feel everything changing. If we'd been physically drawn to one another in the past, we'd success-fully managed to suppress those urges. We never acknowledged them, never did more than exchange awkward kisses on the cheek. But now the temperature was rising—maybe because our circumstances had changed, maybe because we were both so needy. Whatever it was, there was now no denying the heat. The thermometer was about to burst.

I had long desired Karin. I had not seen her for a year, and when she embraced me that night at Peacock Alley, my resolve weakened. I knew that an extramarital affair was the last thing I needed in my al-ready splintered life. I knew that the act of adultery would only darken my guilt-ridden Catholic conscience. But hunger overwhelmed dis-cretion. I tried to resist. I tried to view Karin as simply a potential investor. When she told me she had a small inheritance from her father, I told her about Sassy Curl. Would she be willing to invest five hundred dollars?

"Look, Robert," she said bluntly, "I can't see you as a salesman. I've heard you sing. You have a talent. Why not go back to Aspen for another summer of performances? If you want money to pursue your career, I'll gladly let you have it. But this Sassy Curl scheme is silly, and I don't want anything to do with it."

Her bluntness, her common sense, and mostly her belief in my artistic future, touched me in a place that only fueled my desire. Our friendship was precious to me. I'd never met a woman who under-stood me so deeply. But that friendship was only half-fulfilled. Now its consummation seemed inevitable. Unable to get our moral bear-ings, neither Karin nor I was strong enough to steer clear of the im-pending storm. We became lovers, and, despite tumultuous changes in our individual lives, would remain so for years to follow.

Before Karin, I was naive. I thought I knew satisfying sex when I clearly didn't. Before Karin, sex was pedestrian, due as much to my ineptness as anyone else's. With Karin, the act of making love achieved a relaxed freedom and joy I had never thought possible. Our bodies communicated as well as our minds. We couldn't get enough of each other. Now our union, body and soul, was complete, even as our personal lives spun out of control.

"Our love affair," Karin recalled, "began and continued in secret shame. Before I quit Washington, I'd met Marlene. Bob brought her to a few dinners with our college friends. She was a lovely woman, but always silent and out of place among Bob's sharp-tongued cronies. You could feel trouble brewing between Marlene and Bob. They were incompatible. It pained me to know that our liaison would ultimately hurt her. In the beginning, Bob and I were determined to cut it off. But I soon found myself head over heels in love, and all I could do was go back to New York where I hoped distance would help us forget what had happened."

Jacques, our second son, was born in 1958, another beautiful baby who, like his older brother, Kevin, would prove to have exceptional musical talent. With Karin back in New York, I was out of sorts. Her brief visit to St. Louis and the start of our affair had stirred me in ways that went beyond sex. She had excited me with hope, with the prospect of escaping the doldrums of a noncreative life. We corresponded furiously. Her letters were filled with loving encouragement. "Music," she wrote, "is your fate and your future. It's too late to back down and never too late to go forward."

I thought about it. I'd always been scared of failure. That's why I looked for slam dunks—Geraldine's dress shop, Sassy Curl hair pomade—but slam dunks never happened. I had no interest in law or medicine. I lacked the temperament for teaching. So what was left for me? Music. Only in music did I sense possible success. And only with success came freedom—working according to my own lights, living independently, not being anyone's goddamn servant. Meanwhile, Marlene endured the insecurities I had imposed upon her.

"There was this terrible moment," Marlene recalled, "when Robert came home and asked me to sit with him on the couch. He had something important to tell me. Even before he broke the news, my heart sank. The words he spoke still haunt me. I couldn't express it then—I didn't want to admit it—but I could feel the bottom falling out of our marriage. He said he was going to live in Cleveland, and that, at least for now, there wasn't enough money for me and the boys to join him. He carefully explained what Karamu was all about, why it represented a golden opportunity he couldn't pass up. It seemed logical. But logic didn't stop my mind from reeling: *No,* I thought, *you're not going to leave me the way my mother and stepfather left me; you're not just going to disappear. What about our two babies? What about our life together?* But the thoughts stayed silent, and all I could do was nod my head and say I understood. After all, Robert was older and wiser; he knew what was best. I wanted to be supportive. I wanted to stay strong. I wanted to believe that, once his career kicked off, we'd all be together. So I smiled my best smile, fought back tears, and wished him well. I prayed the move would be good for all of us, but deep inside my heart was crying. My heart feared something I could never express— that once my husband left St. Louis, he'd never return. I had an awful premonition the man was gone for good."

# Karamu

I had every intention of bringing Marlene and the boys to Cleveland as soon as my life was stable, but I knew I'd never return to St. Louis. The city represented everything I sought to escape: jobs that led nowhere, a family background—and especially a mother—that provoked feelings of pain and confusion, and an increasing temptation to lead the life of a hustler. I saw Cleveland as a life saver. I was desperate to change my fortune, control my fate, and make it in a brave new world I both desired and feared.

I feared failure. The fear was so acute I hid it under a facade of sophistication and cockiness. I did such a good job that I hid the fear from myself. For the first time in my life, I was living outside the city of my birth. The notion of a new locale energized me, drove me into the reservoir of ambition that, as I'd learn in these coming years, was an essential part of my personality. In my early thirties, I already felt, as the poet put it, "time's winged chariot hurrying near." In one form or another, I wanted success. Karamu had been an established community center for some thirty-five years, providing blacks with a chance to hone theatrical skills. If I were to make something of myself, I desperately needed those skills. I was determined, but also lonely as hell.

Karin and I carried on a heated correspondence. I took the money she gave me and turned it over to Marlene. Karin's position was simple—if doing that freed my mind to make the move to Cleveland, she was glad. She wished me well. She believed in my talent and wanted nothing to hold me back. Karin saw that for me, like her, St. Louis was a roadblock. She was thrilled that I had escaped it and resolved to leave me alone. But when her letters arrived, reminding me of everything we shared, our resolve melted. Passion—pure sexual longing—certainly played a part. Our physical connection was powerful. But just as powerful was our emotional and intellectual connection. We were soul mates. She said it, I said it, and soon we were discussing how and when we would get together. Because Karamu had already given me a big role—Billy Bigelow in *Carousel*—it made no sense for me to leave Cleveland. But did it make sense for Karin to leave New York? "If you come here," I wrote, "I can't make any promises. I long to see you and be with you, but I'm afraid that longing may be selfish. You'll have to do what's best for you." "You'll have to say whether you really want me there," she wrote back. "Of course I do," I answered. "I'd be lying to say otherwise. Nothing would bring me greater pleasure." Finally, nothing stopped us—not restraint, not fear of the unknown, not the notion of a white woman moving in with a married black man. Love led the way. Love, I was convinced, would see us through.

I loved Karin, no doubt; and I loved the idea of her moving to Cleveland, even as I was thrown into further guilt concerning the family I had left in St. Louis. For three months, I had lived alone in a furnished room. A live-in girlfriend who was not only bright and beautiful but wholeheartedly supported my career seemed a gift from the gods I was incapable of refusing. When she arrived, we pooled our resources and found a pleasant one-bedroom apartment. Karin worked as a typesetter. I got several jobs. The first was in a warehouse, unloading and stocking Christmas lights. The second was at Sligo Iron and Steel, a gig I had to quit when the paint fumes tore up my singing voice. The third was at Cleveland State Hospital. I cared for patients in the nonviolent mental ward, helping to bathe and feed them. I liked this job best because it gave me a sense of helping others. I was touched by the benign nature of those who had fallen into emotional disarray. Among those was a famous basketball player, a wizard on the court who had dazzled crowds throughout the world.

To see this great athlete—alone, afraid, and reduced to the docility of a small child—touched my heart. It was a privilege to serve him lunch. My pay was only fifteen dollars a week, but the rewards were more than monetary.

My main work, of course, was at Karamu. At the risk of sounding conceited, I was seen as someone with a degree of musical maturity. Lead roles came my way. My age might have helped. I was older than most of my colleagues. Ron O'Neal, for instance, who later gained fame as Superfly, was ten years my junior. Ron was a brilliant thespian and strong vocalist. He had the looks and charisma of a movie star. We became running partners, and because of the age difference, he saw me as something of a mentor, a new role for me. More than ever, I was an opinionated son-of-a-bitch, whether I knew what I was talking about or not. Ron and I shared a seriousness about legitimate acting and an appreciation of beautiful women. Our friendship grew over the years, and our careers, in fascinating juxtaposition, ran along parallel tracks.

Although the Karamu productions were sparse—our only musical accompaniment was piano—the pieces, such as Carlisle Floyd's superb opera *Susannah,* were demanding. I benefited from the lessons of stage director Benno Frank. An Israeli in his sixties, Benno was old school. He had worked at the Habima, the national theater of Israel, and had no interest in psychological subtleties or fashionable notions of Method acting. "White people," he would tell us black actors, "may need a method to find their feelings. You have no such problems." Instead, his direction was absolutely utilitarian. Forty years later, they are directions I still employ. Benno was not the world's most charming man. He tended to spit rather than talk. As he barked out orders, tobacco juice dribbled down his cheek. None of this endeared him to the women. But I related to his hard-nosed manner. I knew I needed to learn the basics, and the basics—verbalized in no-nonsense terms that even a hardhead like myself could not ignore—were articulated by Benno Frank night after night:

*Speak clearly.*
*Speak louder; I can't hear you.*
*Speak softer; you're shouting.*
*Don't bump into the furniture.*
*Enter when it's time to enter.*
*Exit when it's time to exit.*

Benno broke down the basics to their absolute essence. If he thought you had not learned your lines or carried out his directions, he'd throw you out on your ass—no apologies offered. After years of high-minded intellectual debate with professors back in St. Louis, I was ready for someone to cut through my bullshit. "Guillaume," he'd say, "stand in the goddamn light or get off the goddamn stage!"

Cleveland was where I traded Robert Williams in for Robert Guillaume. A new city, a new career, a new name—it all made sense. Reinventing myself, losing the loser who never got anywhere in St. Louis required radical rechristening. Robert Williams was too common a name. Besides, I knew of several Robert Williamses on death row. In choosing a name, I wanted something distinctive. I thought Frenchifying Williams into Guillaume was a classy move. I had taken second-year French and heard Guillaume as a cinch to pronounce. I was wrong. My self-invented name has been mangled more than I could have ever imagined. Perhaps it served me right; perhaps it's the price I've paid for my pretentiousness. Further down the dusty road of my career, when I tried my hand at stand-up comedy, I used my name as a source of self-ridicule. "It's not pronounced Giggly-yum," I told the audience, "or Guy-you-me. It's Guillaume, an old noble French name going back to my great-great-great grandfather Kunte Guillaume and his brother Bubba Guillaume."

Back in the late fifties, I saw no humor in the name change. I was serious about cutting myself off from the past. It was one thing, though, to ignore my family of origin, but another to forget the family of my own making. Marlene and the boys were always on my mind. They were the reason that Karin left Cleveland. It was an agonizing break. As a live-in couple, Karin and I had proven to be wonderfully compatible. Karin saw how professional instruction had resulted in my artistic growth. Interracial couples were still an anomaly, but given the liberal atmosphere of Karamu, we were accepted. There was a strong aura of optimism. My colleagues and I used to say, "We're changing the world." I couldn't help but be affected by the idealism. Idealism was part of Karin's own nature. Ours was an idealistic love. But conspiring against all this good feeling was the obligation I felt toward my family. The boys were babies, and Marlene was dependent on what little money I could send. Should I send for her? Karin never argued against such a move. When I finally wrote Marlene and asked her to make the trip with the boys, Karin bowed out. There were tears and anguish, but Karin encouraged my attempt at reconciliation. She went back to New York, convinced our troubled affair was finally at an end.

"I arrived with the boys for a visit," Marlene remembered. "I was glad Bob was doing well at the theater. At the same time, I also felt him disconnecting himself from me. There was talk of our remaining, but I sensed that wasn't what he wanted. He wanted to be left alone to pursue his career. Our visit was short and not very satisfying. We went back to St. Louis with only a vague idea of reuniting with him, someplace, somehow. I knew he adored Kevin and Jacques. But I also knew his life was headed in a different direction."

My life was suddenly simplified to living alone. If loneliness was part of my daily grind, I was not about to admit it. Stoicism was my style. My wife, my lover, my sons—I managed to avoid dwelling on what was missing and concentrate on learning the lessons of Benno Frank. *Get on stage when it's time to get on; get off when it's time to get off.* Life's stage directions were not quite as clear.

On any given evening, after rehearsal or performance, I might go out for beers with Ron O'Neal. He was good company. He displayed keen interest not only in serious drama, but in the drama of the streets as well. Ron had come up in Cleveland and knew his way around.

He admired the style and savvy of the pimps—perhaps we all did—
even as he understood the subtleties of characters created by George
Bernard Shaw and William Shakespeare. We'd plot the course of our
careers like playwrights concocting dramas. I'd wind up singing *La
Boheme* at the Met. Ron would play Hamlet on the London stage.
Enough beers and we'd be convinced.

Convincing evidence concerning my career arrived unexpectedly.
It happened after I'd been in Cleveland for a year. Howard Roberts, a
Karamu alumnus, returned to his alma mater to find talent for a musical he was mounting. Roberts was a fine musician—he and Alvin
Ailey collaborated on *Revelations*—with a national reputation. The
show for which he was musical director, *Free and Easy*, concerned
black jockeys at the turn of the century and required a large cast. The
production starred Harold Nicholas of the famed Nicholas Brothers.
Rehearsals were set for New York; the company would go on a six-
month European tour then return to the Palace Theater on Broadway,
where Sammy Davis, Jr., would replace Nicholas and then take the
show to the London Palladium. As we heard this dazzling litany of
places and names, our heartbeats quickened. We were terribly eager.
Over a period of days, Roberts scrupulously auditioned the members of our company and selected three: Beverly Todd, my costar in
*Carousel*, Gwen Walters, who played "Susannah," and myself.

"Guillaume," he asked, "how soon can you be in New York?"

"Mr. Roberts," I replied, "I'm already there."

# The City

I lived in New York some seventeen years, yet hardly felt myself a New Yorker. I was always an outsider, just as I had been in St. Louis and Cleveland, just as I would be in Vienna and Tel Aviv. I arrived in the city at the dawn of the sixties and, if you asked me, would underplay my impression of the great metropolis. Oohing and aahing, even at an urban colossus as mighty as Manhattan, was not my style. I affected indifference. I stuck with the specifics of the city's geography. I read the grids and walked accordingly. Uptown, downtown, east and west. The signs were plain, the numbers logical, the subway direct and cheap. I kept both feet on the ground. But if I acted not in the least intimidated by these super-sophisticated new surroundings, I gave myself away when, minutes after my arrival, I called the one person whose emotional support I desperately sought: Karin Berg.

She was living with friends on 110th Street when I suddenly showed up. Despite everything that happened, we were thrilled—we had missed one another and still wanted to be together. Karin told me I was strong enough to take on the city and win. She believed in my future more than I did. I needed her confidence. I was happy to move in with her friends, Ruth and Al LaRocca, happy to sleep on their floor with Karin. I'd walk over to 112th and Amsterdam, where I found the world's largest cathedral, St. John the Divine, awe inspiring. Its architectural intricacies and interconnections had me considering the interconnections in my own life. My connection to Karin was never more important. I was comforted by her familiarity with the city. If, in my secret heart, I found New York unapproachable, Karin harbored no such fear. She had already mastered its mazes. She haunted the clubs in Greenwich Village—the Vanguard, the Gate, the Five Spot—and had secured a support system among jazz aficionados. I shared her appreciation, if not her passion, for the modernity of Miles and Monk. My concentration, though, was on *Free and Easy*.

I played the Conjur Man, a small role with a small song. The production itself was enormous, involving some eighty-five people and Quincy Jones's band. It was a lively spectacle, a rehash of an earlier piece starring Pearl Bailey. Producer Stanley Chase, coming off a smash with Bertolt Brecht's *Three Penny Opera*, harbored high hopes. He had sunk $350,000, a fortune back then, into the show and expected we would conquer the world.

I had notions of conquering my guilt. When I learned that we would be playing Paris directly after New York rehearsals, I urged Marlene to join me there. Other married men in the company—the fine tenor Paul Jackson, for example—were bringing their families, and it seemed a perfect way to reunite mine. Marlene deliberated but finally refused. I couldn't blame her. Because I had deserted her once, she had no assurance that I wouldn't do it again. The life I was living seemed precarious to her. She thought Kevin and Jacques needed stability. I also believe that people close to her in St. Louis had long ago lost faith in my goodwill. Moreover, my selling job was half-hearted.

Paris pleased me. I have a facility for language and, though I could have done more with my French, I got by. I felt free in Europe. Europeans were certainly not free of racial bias, but ongoing racial tension, so much a part of American life, was noticeably absent. On the other hand, here we were presenting Europeans with an all-black musical revue set in an earlier epoch, a piece that did nothing to contradict their notion of African Americans as lighthearted, fun-loving entertainers. It would be one of the great ironies of my career that, over and again, such roles and productions would come my way. As a survivor, as someone determined to make it in a cold-blooded business, I took whatever decent work I could find. But that didn't keep me from expressing opinions and attitudes.

During my first European trip, my emotional attitude was peculiar: I was delighted to wander through the Louvre and sit in Left Bank cafés; yet, part of me had presumed that, once I left St. Louis, wonderful things would happen. These were places I'd always heard about, and now I was there. None of the Parisian sights, though, impressed as much as the talent of Harold Nicholas.

Harold turned us all into raving fans. He was extraordinary. Even though operatic stars like Jussi Björling and Roland Hayes remained my role models, Nicholas showed me the absolute genius of mainstream African American entertainment. As a dancer, his athleticism was not only a physical wonder, but a work of sublime art. In *Free and Easy*, there was a section when several couples strut the stage doing the cakewalk. I was among them. My dancing skills are rudimentary at best, but my partner and I took pride in several nifty moves. Harold would "answer" each couple's cakewalk with his own improvised version. Watching him, we would melt. Our jaws would drop. The man didn't merely dance; he flew. Harold was extravagantly talented—arguably as talented as Sammy. But unlike Sammy, Harold could never play second banana to a Frank Sinatra. Harold couldn't play second banana to anyone. After all, he'd been a film star. He could sing; he could dance his ass off; he could carry a show on his shoulders. Harold Nicholas was a bad motherfucker and didn't mind letting you know. Call it arrogance; call it confidence. Whatever you call it, I liked it. It was privilege to work in his shadow.

Despite dynamic dancing and singing, *Free and Easy* failed. Four months in three cities—Paris, Brussels, and Amsterdam—was all she wrote. The box office was lackluster and the producer out of money. We never opened in New York, and Sammy never joined the company. I was back in the city, disappointed that the run had not been longer but, more than ever, determined to hang in. I had had my first taste of the big time, and I liked it. The idea of reuniting my family— their moving to New York or my returning home—was no longer an option. Marlene didn't mention it, and neither did I. We remained married because, well, we were Catholics, and Catholics don't divorce. I also think marriage protected me from other commitments. I was free and not free at the same time. There was nothing to interfere with my relationship with Karin. Finally we could settle down and live together in peace—or so I thought. We found an apartment at 358 West Twenty-ninth Street and set up house.

Were it not for Karin, I would not have survived those early years in New York. She was my shelter in the storm. She offered me unconditional love and unconditional support. When my twelfth straight audition led nowhere, she assured me thirteen would be my lucky number. When my lowly job in the garment district couldn't pay my share of the rent, Karin supplied the rest. And she did so with good cheer and grace. Never was I made to feel guilty. Never was I chastised for underearning or underachieving.

"Bob was a worker," said Karin. "Even when he wasn't working, he was working to find work. His work ethic never waned. I was a little bit more employable. My secretarial skills were always in demand. But I was also going through a transition of my own. I was beginning to see myself as a writer. I began toying with music journalism and expanding my literary interests. I was moved by Doris Lessing's *Golden Notebook*. Lessing's portrait of a woman struggling for her autonomy was an early feminist wake-up call. For all his erudition, Bob refused to read the book. But in any other areas, he was ahead of the curve. When I started to scrub the floor, for example, he got down on his hands and knees and joined me. 'I live here, too,' he said. 'The dirty work is as much mine as yours.'"

As a couple, Karin and I enjoyed an insular domesticity. I relished our home life. Aside from work, I wasn't much on going out. The naked truth is that, as part of a racially mixed couple, I was far from comfortable. Imagine us—a dark-skinned black and a Scandinavian blond—walking the streets of the city. The visual impact was powerful, the shock value unnerving. Manhattan's liberalism did not preclude deep-seated bigotry, especially in the early days of the civil rights movement. I was not interested in incidents or dirty looks. Maybe because I feared my temper, I avoided situations in which we risked being scorned. Or maybe I was ashamed; maybe I lacked the guts of a racial pioneer. Either way, I stayed home. Karin would prove to be a political activist; I never was. Socially, I was the square and Karin the hipster. She was conversant with the counterculture—the beat literature, for example, of Allen Ginsberg and Jack Kerouac— and felt a part of the artistic avant-garde. I did not. My eye was still on the Met.

"Bob would have made the Met had he not been a romantic tenor," Karin believed. "Black baritones had a better chance because they're usually not the sexual pivot of the opera. A lyric tenor is a leading man. This was a time when few leading men were black."

I'd like to agree with Karin and view my failure as the result of racism. Racism may have contributed. Racism is a pernicious and difficult strain to isolate. But it wasn't racism that kept me out of the Met. The timbre of my voice did me in, not the color of my skin. On one occasion I made an impression on a conductor. I bowled him over. That morning I somehow employed a muscularity that delivered the right sound. "Come back at three," he said excitedly, "and sing for my full staff." By three, I had lost what I had found. The sound was gone. I oversang, a defect that would follow me for decades. My mind had shifted, my sense of dynamics dissipated. The same story unfolded when I actually auditioned for the Met. I sang "Amor ti vieta" from Giordano's *Fedora*. The aria is standard repertoire, dramatic and short. It requires some subtlety. I had none. Opera also requires a certain texture that I lacked. I'm not trying to be overly modest. My voice was strong, my pitch reliable. Yet, as a friend once put it, I sounded like a loud folk singer, not a sensitive interpreter of the nineteenth-century *lirica*. Anyway, I had neither the time nor inclination to cry over spilled milk. I needed work and, with that in mind, retreated to Broadway.

In pursuing work, I had the tenacity of a hungry junkyard dog. No matter the number of rejections, I kept coming back. Every day I studied the bulletin board at Equity. When a new show put out their audition notice, I was there. Every time. Some auditions allowed me to choose the material. I was partial to "Without a Song." I'd start singing, "Without a song, the day will never end . . ." and suddenly be dismissed with a curt "Next!" Frustrated, I finally figured a way to put my best foot forward by starting at the chorus—"I'll get along as long as the song is strong in my *soul.*" "*Soul*" was sung on the high note that demonstrated my lung power. At the very least, they would hear my high note and feel my soul.

Early in the sixties, as my career began to gain some steam, I sang in the City Center's production of *Porgy and Bess.* Thus began a ten-year relationship with this winsome, troublesome piece of Americana. I was employed as the understudy for Sportin' Life, a nefarious but charming character. Mainly, though, I sang with fifteen other men and sixteen women in the chorus. Even then, my attitude about the folk opera was ambivalent. I had some notion of its history. When George Gershwin wrote it in the thirties, there was no outcry that the piece patronizes blacks or that its characters are stereotypes who appear, in my view, as niggers, not Negroes. Black men did not fail to note that Porgy, the romantic hero, is without legs, his sexuality thus eliminated. Sidney Poitier, coerced by Sam Goldwyn into playing Porgy in the 1958 film with Dorothy Dandridge, wrote in his autobiography, *This Life,* "*Porgy and Bess* was not material complimentary to black people; and for the most part, black people responded negatively to that American opera, although they stood ready to acknowledge and applaud the genius in the music." I agree. The piece has survived but only through the sublimity of its score.

I knew that three distinguished personalities—John W. Bubbles, Cab Calloway, and Sammy Davis, Jr.—had played Sportin' Life to great acclaim. I also knew of the legendary productions—the 1935 version with Todd Duncan and Anne Brown and the touring company that crossed the country in the fifties with Leontyne Price and William Warfield. Laverne Hutcherson had also played Porgy. One of the great tenors of his day, Hutcherson hailed from St. Louis and performed the role there in 1952; I, then twenty-five years old, socialized with him and members of the cast. As we sat around, I argued interpretation with all the overwrought passion of brazen youth. Hutcherson's glorious voice made a deep impression. Years later, when I saw him working as an attendant in the men's room of a New York deli, I was shocked and saddened. I needed no further proof of the precariousness of a black man's career on the legit stage.

That precariousness added to my ambivalence about *Porgy and Bess.* Serious black singers need work, and the play has consistently provided blacks with that work since its debut. I am grateful. I was grateful in the early sixties when I found myself in the chorus. But that didn't stop me, and my choir chronies, from deriding the piece. We saw ourselves as young Turks, storming the gates. Given the shift in racial attitudes from the thirties to the sixties, the drama invoked an ambience many of us no longer found palatable. If anything, on opening night at City Center, we were condescending about a play we considered condescending. We were feeling our vocal power; we had an enormous sound; our harmonies were spectacularly rich; but we sure as hell weren't going to get caught up in this sentimental story of a cripple and his no 'count woman. We regarded the melodrama with disdain. And no moment is more melodramatic than when, at the end, Porgy emerges from jail to learn Bess has fled. Unhesitatingly, he demands, "Bring my goat." The women want to know where he's going. "Up North," he says. "Where up North?" they ask. "Way past the custom house," he answers before breaking into song. "Oh Lord," he sings, "I'm on my way. On my way to a heavenly land." The choir joins in. "I'm on my way," we sing. "On my way" becomes a melodic mantra, a crescendo of feverish excitement and improbable optimism. In rehearsal, we viewed this climax as banal. But now, with the audience leaping to its feet and cheering like mad, I felt my eyes filling with tears. I was embarrassed until I saw that my fellow singers were teary-eyed as well. Our cynicism dissolved. What had seemed silly yesterday smacked of absolute truth today. Moreover, the music is among the most affecting I have ever heard.

There are other marvels to be gleaned from *Porgy*. "Summertime," "I Loves You Porgy," "Bess, You Is My Woman," "It Ain't Necessarily So"—Gershwin's gift for melody was rare. His synthesis of jazzy rhythms and operatic motifs was brilliant. Taken in its entirety, though, the piece needs pruning. Too many silly songs detract from the great ones. But no matter how one criticizes the racial attitudes, the music endures. I think back forty years to when I first sang it, when we young warriors in the chorus were still certain we'd crack the Met. Those of us who found fault with the opera would have rejoiced nonetheless if it *had* been performed at the Met. That would have made our entrance easier. Sadly, that didn't happen until 1985.

Not much was happening for blacks on Broadway in the early sixties. Given so few productions, I was lucky to nab as many gigs as I did. My first real break was the musical *Kwamina*. It opened in October 1961, at the Fifty-fourth Street Theater, the same venue where *Porgy and Bess* had opened in 1935, and ran for thirty-two performances. Music and lyrics were by Richard Adler; it was his first attempt to write solo after the death of his partner, Jerry Ross, with whom he'd created *Damn Yankees* and *The Pajama Game*. The book was by Robert Alan Aurther. The action takes place in a West African village on the eve of its independence. The production, which tried out in Toronto before moving to Broadway, was splashy. I had a good supporting role, lots of lines, and considerable singing.

Bobby Lewis, a founder of the Actor's Studio, was the director. He believed in the Method. Unfortunately, I had no method. I'd been feeling fortunate that, so soon after arriving in New York, I'd landed a Broadway musical. But if I had any notions of grandiosity, Lewis destroyed them. Perhaps justifiably. In the key scene, in which my lover dies, I couldn't convey any emotion Lewis found credible. He thought my performance was phony, that I lacked rudimentary acting skills. He was right. I tried unsuccessfully to satisfy his direction. Only the fact that my understudy was a lousy singer and an even worse actor saved me.

My struggle paled next to the warfare between Adler and Aurther. Adler was married to Sally Anne Howes, who played the white nurse working in the African village's clinic. Aurther's story is focused on the interracial romance between Howes and Terry Carter, a black doctor recently returned to that village from England. Adler complained that the romance was too explicit. Aurther argued the romance was the whole ticket. Adler wanted the music to imply their attraction; Aurther was hell-bent on *showing* that attraction. The cast was sure Adler simply didn't want his wife embracing a black man. The dispute raged on until the men, right in front of the King Edward Hotel in Toronto, traded blows. The producer pulled them apart. "Gentlemen, gentlemen," he urged, "this must be resolved in a civilized manner." By the time we opened in New York, the resolution was clear: the white woman is never touched by the black man; even an innocent onstage kiss is purged from the action.

Even if I denounced the racial attitude that prevented a public kiss, the same attitude affected my private life. The bond between Karin and me remained private. Of course our close chums knew of our involvement, but I sure as hell didn't send announcements to family and friends back home. For her part, Karin was content was to let me pursue my career without demands. She required no commitment. In fact, she provided the ongoing encouragement I found so sustaining. She alone understood that, given my strange temperament, I was pursuing the one goal that might provide me with what I had long sought—independence. I saw the stage—if not the Met then the Broadway stage—as the single place where I could be myself. I was dead set on maintaining whatever I considered my dignity. If you had asked me to define the term, my answer might have been muddled. But in my gut I knew what I wanted: I did not want to be looked down upon; I did not what to ass-kiss; I did not want to be told what to do—or how to act.

# Acting as Though

Acting as though I wasn't afraid, acting as though my life depended upon getting theatrical work, acting as though I could never go back to bus driving or dishwashing or Sassy Curl selling, acting as though I was perfectly suited for every role I attempted, acting as though the future was ripe with possibilities and good fortune just around the corner—this was my great act in those years. Acting as though I knew what the hell I was doing.

Maybe it was my seeming self-assurance, maybe my loud voice, maybe my straight-ahead acting style. Whatever it was, I landed roles on a surprisingly consistent basis. *Fly, Blackbird* was another musical revue, this one off-Broadway. It had originated in L. A. with Al Freeman, whose role I assumed when the production came to New York. The play was successful enough to merit a cast recording by Mercury Records. The cast included Avon Long, one of the first actors to play Sportin' Life in *Porgy and Bess,* and Jim Bailey, who later gained fame as a female impersonator. The theme was student sit-ins. Although I was thirty-five, the producers thought I could pass for twenty-one and cast me as the student leader. In theater I became an activist, a role I eschewed in real life. I approached real life in the theater in strictly practical terms. I was an actor for hire. If I could bring enough authenticity to a role to elicit an offer, I took it.

Working in *Tambourines to Glory,* a musical based on Langston Hughes's novel, was another instance of the disparity between the real and the theatrical that had me, a Catholic boy, toiling in Baptist fields. I loved Hughes's poems and plays; I revered him as a key contributor to the Harlem Renaissance. His ear for the language of his people was unerring; his wit was biting and his literary sensibility singularly black. So was this musical. *Tambourines* starred Clara Ward of the world-famous Ward Singers. Aretha Franklin's primary inspiration, Ward was viewed, along with Mahalia Jackson, as one of the great voices in gospel. Because Hughes's piece was set in a fundamentalist congregation, she was the perfect choice. Her performance delivered all the emotional theatrics white audiences associate with black churches. My own association, however, was not extremely positive. Hearing Ward, I couldn't deny the passion of her style; nor could I keep my mind from returning to a scene straight out of my St. Louis childhood:

*I'm nine, maybe ten years old. Grandma is taking me to Mass. She has me dressed in a little Lord Fauntleroy suit; she's holding my hand, explaining the importance of taking communion. Not far from our house, we pass by a small church making loud music. The sign on the front says Mt. Olive Baptist. The sounds reaching the street are overwhelming, raucous, intriguing. It sounds like a party. I know there are black people inside, but have no idea what they're doing. Grandma senses my curiosity. "I'll show you this one time," she says, "and that will be it." She holds my hand a little tighter as we walk up the steps and open the front door to the church. Music smacks me in the face, music more emotional and freewheeling than any I've ever encountered. Compared to the solemnity of the Catholic mass, I can't believe this is church. Can't believe the way people are dancing in the aisles; can't believe the exaltations of the preacher, can't believe the congregation shouting back at him, the women passing out, the nurses applying smelling salts, the choir shouting, "Feel a little wheel a-turning . . . I know young hearts are burning . . . have a little talk with Jesus . . . Good God Almighty, a little talk with Jesus . . . turning turning turning. . . ." The place is rocking, walls shaking, wooden floor planks rumbling underneath the stomping. At one point, I grow a little frightened. Is this religion or is this a riot? "Now you see," says Grandma, "why I don't want you in churches like this."*

I saw my roots before, in fact, I knew they were my roots. Grandma saw the elements of such worship as rituals of the past. She was convinced that my future rested in superseding such rituals. Civility meant Catholicism. The Baptists were too boisterous, too black. I don't like admitting that I absorbed such attitudes, but I did. The practical side of me fought the prejudice. I auditioned and won the lead in *Tambourines to Glory*. Later, Lou Gossett, a better-known actor than I, took over while I assumed a lesser role. I didn't mind. I kept top billing and sang a pleasing song, "Moon outside My Window." I was pleased to be part of anything that paid. I only wish my background had permitted me to appreciate Clara Ward's genius. Today I can do so. Back then, I was still struggling with my past.

That past was sometimes misinterpreted. During the run of *Tambourines*, John Hammond, the famous blues and jazz producer, became enamored of my talent. Hammond was an executive at Columbia Records who had signed Count Basie, Billie Holiday, and Aretha Franklin. He would later sign Bob Dylan and Bruce Springsteen. Hammond mistakenly saw me as a musical primitive. He thought I could sing gospel or perhaps even jazz. I was flattered but then not at all surprised when his interest waned. The minute Hammond realized I was not going to be the next Joe Williams or Big Bill Broonzy, he dropped out of sight.

The question of musical versatility, however, remained vital. If I were to survive, I'd have to sing in several styles. Gutbucket blues or jazz scat might not work for me, but there were nightclubs that featured material more to my liking. In between stage engagements, clubs were an important source of employment. New York City was full of clubs. The Exodus, at Sixty-ninth and Broadway, hired me to sing on weekends. My repertoire consisted of popular numbers from current musicals, for example, "If Ever I Should Leave You" from *Camelot*, "Sunrise, Sunset" from *Fiddler on the Roof*. In those days, many of us took our cue from Harry Belafonte and included

Israeli folk songs in our repertoire. Yiddish numbers were also obvious favorites with the largely Jewish audience. A fellow singer, Mort Freeman, was kind enough to teach me a group of such songs. In the light of the emerging civil rights movement, at a time when integration was celebrated, hearing a black man singing Yiddish with authentic pronunciation pleased any number of liberal New Yorkers. My mixed feelings about the matter only became more mixed when I started working the Catskills.

The Catskills, of course, is the resort area north of New York City sometimes called the Borscht Belt. Dozens of hotels in sylvan settings offer outdoor recreation, live entertainment, and abundant food. (One of the first Catskills jokes I heard was, "Back home in Brooklyn, Bessie tells her neighbor, 'The food was lousy—and there wasn't enough.'") The list of legendary Catskills comics, from Jack Benny to Jerry Lewis, is long. The customers were overwhelmingly Jewish. The Catskills has a history of liberalism. Left-wingers flocked there; socialist camps were common; and the atmosphere was highly political. At various times, I felt both pleased and patronized by such attitudes.

I was only marginally successful in the Catskills. I worked at Maude's Bungalow Colony, for example, owned by the Slutsky family, well-known left-wingers, who treated me with affection. My song selection was typically eclectic—"They Call the Wind Mariah," "You Make Me Feel So Young," "O Sole Mio." I'd throw in a Yiddish number or two, but when it came to the perennial favorite, "My Yiddishe Mama," made famous by Sophie Tucker, I refused. Pleasing the audience was one thing, but pleasing myself came first. The sentiment of "My Yiddishe Mama" coming out of the mouth of a black man struck me as inauthentic. My ambivalence was never more apparent: I wanted to succeed, but only on my own terms. When I felt those terms being dictated, I bucked.

The collegial atmosphere of the Catskills was stimulating. My opinion was often sought on a range of topics, and, though I declaimed as best I could, I frequently felt intellectually outclassed. That made me declaim even more. The place was also rife with romance. The secluded bungalows, moonlit lakes, and secret groves were all well suited to sexual intrigue. Willing white women offered temptations I made little effort to resist. Liberal politics and liberal sex went hand in hand. Given the illegitimacy of my situation with Karin—I was still, after all, married to Marlene—monogamy made no sense. At least that was my rationalization. In my mind, I was free to do as I pleased.

Other entertainers conquered the Catskills. I never did. I think my ambivalence about being a Negro on display for open-minded liberals was all too apparent. I also think I read the audience wrong. I remember once telling a Jewish joke during a performance, certain it would hit the right chord. The audience reacted with cold silence. Afterward, a sympathetic customer told me the joke was best told by a Jew, not a black. I presumed an intimacy I did not have. Conversely, when whites assumed they understood my emotional dilemmas as a black man, I'd go off. My temper was explosive. I remained an indefatigable debater. I had to be right and, in that pursuit, was as tiresome as ever. When friends reminded me of that character flaw, I sometimes heard them and sometimes didn't. Only a fool would ignore the fact that charm is essential to success in show business. One must charm the audience; one must charm one's associates, one's manager, one's booking agent. I was not without such charm. I had a good smile, a decent wit, a cordiality, a conversational ease. Then why was I so often blatantly uncharming and contentious? Something still smoldered within my soul. I couldn't name it. I'm not sure I understood it. But it was there. Like oil and water, my drive and my defiance did not mix.

"We were living in radical times," Karin remembered, "our relationship was certainly affected. My own radicalization happened during the civil rights era. I became an activist. Bob didn't. I'm glad he didn't because, given his temperament, he could not have contained himself in the nonviolent arena. I remember one night we were watching the news. A hippie child, a teenaged boy, burned his draft card while the cops beat him unmercifully. Bob went ballistic. The innocence of the boy and the brutality of the police just got to him. Bob hollered, pounded the table, did everything but put his fist through the screen. It made me realize how dangerous he would have been on the front lines. His righteous indignation would not have helped the cause."

The cause deepened Karin's sense of purpose. She went to nonviolent workshops and traveled south on the Freedom Rides. In the summer of 1964, when Freedom Riders Michael Schwerner, Andrew Goodman, and James Chaney were murdered on a lonely road in Mississippi, a dark shadow was cast over the mission. Their martyrdom strengthened Karin's resolve. She was active in the Congress of Racial Equality (CORE) and the Committee to Employ Negro Performers (CENP), which operated in New York. I had problems with CENP. I thought it operated out of psychological timidity; I saw it as actors going to employers with hat in hand. No matter how desperate I was to work, I could never beg.

My list of credits makes it sound like I was working more than I was. I found work, to be sure, but there were long periods of downtime, during which unemployment checks kept me in corn flakes. The fact that Karin had found work—and purpose—in the civil rights struggle made me proud. She was indomitable. She was also feisty and fearless. Fearlessness is not a quality I could claim. I applauded her efforts but was too frightened to enter the fray. I'd like to say that I chose not to accompany Karin to Mississippi out of high principle, perhaps an affinity for Malcolm X's philosophy rather than Martin Luther King's. While I admired Malcolm's thought, the truth is that I recognized the wise pragmatism that informed King's approach. I didn't go because I was afraid of being killed. I may have also been afraid of losing my cool and strangling a redneck. But my greater fear was that some redneck would strangle me.

I take no pride in confessing to sitting out the great social, political, and moral movement of my time. I'd like to portray my lack of involvement in a better light. I cannot. My actions were centered on myself. I wanted to survive; I wanted to make it; I wanted work. My obsession to succeed overshadowed all else. I felt the tumult. I knew I was living in historically significant times. But nothing was as significant as avoiding personal failure. In my early years, I had experienced enough failure to last a lifetime. Now I was thirty-eight, I was approaching middle age, and I was dead-set on breaking through one way or another.

# Golden Opportunities

The early sixties on Broadway were all about Dick Van Dyke in *Bye Bye Birdie*, Julie Andrews in *Camelot*, Robert Morse in *How to Succeed in Business without Really Trying*, Carol Channing in *Hello, Dolly!* Barbra Streisand in *Funny Girl*, and Zero Mostel in *Fiddler on the Roof*. It was a white, white world. There were a few anomalies. After seeing Diahann Carroll on the *Jack Paar Show*, Richard Rodgers was persuaded to write a musical around her talents. *No Strings* became the vehicle and Diahann became a star. Black actors stalking Broadway for work saw the success of *No Strings* as a sign things might be improving. Two years later, in the fall of 1964, *Golden Boy* opened at the Majestic with Sammy Davis in the lead. The piece was based on Clifford Odets's play from 1937. Odets was brought in to write the libretto in which the hero, an Italian-American, is transformed into a black boxer fighting to break out of Harlem. A Harlem native, Sammy understood the metaphor. At that point, Sammy's fame was at its height; he'd been anointed by Sinatra and recognized as a crown prince of American entertainment. Sammy had run with the Rat Pack, marched with Dr. King, proven his mettle as brilliant dancer, singer, comic, and actor. This was his chance to conquer Broadway.

The conquest was not easy. Odets died during the production's early stages and problems ensued. The critics were not kind. But Sammy was committed, and even when it looked like an early closing was inevitable, he turned back the tide by virtue of his steely tenacity. He simply wouldn't accept failure. He poured his huge heart into keeping the musical alive until it finally found an audience. When I was asked to join the company, *Golden Boy* had been running for nearly a year, a tribute to Sammy's irrepressible spirit. We black actors, operating along the margins of full employment, were bolstered by Sammy's example. We held him in awe. He had the perseverance and power to keep a company together in which we might find work. Beyond that, he had enough electricity to light up all five boroughs. Charisma is one thing; many actors have it. But Sammy had a kind of cosmic charisma that gave the term new meaning.

This is the arena in which I arrived to play Sammy's brother, a small part. More important, I also understudied the second lead, Lou Gossett, who played Eddie Satin, the Golden Boy's slick manager. Billy Daniels, famous for "That Old Black Magic," had originated the role. When Lou missed a couple of performances, I stepped in. That meant I would have a number of dramatic moments on stage with Sammy. This was my big chance.

I blew it. Strange, because I blew it without even knowing I had blown it. As an actor—and as a man—my sensitivity was woefully underdeveloped. I was excited to join the company. Never before had I appeared in such a high-profile production. In addition to Sammy and Lou, Lola Falana was in the cast. The songs were stirring. I was eager to prove my mettle, and the first time I played Eddie Satin, I was ready. I knew the lines, the lyrics, the stage moves. In the big scene where Eddie reamed out Sammy and broke into song—"this is the life . . . here's where the living is"—the drama was intense. Sammy and I were deep into a duet. The problem, though, was that Sammy's microphone went dead. Mine was working just fine, so I carried on as though nothing had happened. At the time I saw this as the professional course of action. The audience could hear me while Sammy was practically inaudible. Another entertainer might have graciously lowered the volume of his singing. But that wasn't me. I belted it out. I later recognized that by virtue of my behavior, I was saying to the star, *Your problems have nothing to do with me.*

Sammy never said a word to me. He treated me well, and I'd like to say we became friends. We did, but much later in life. At that point

I was too intimidated to approach him on a personal level. Besides, if anything hip was happening, Sammy was part of it. I was far from hip. Now I see—then I didn't—that I felt inferior. Sammy moved in a world that felt too fast, too extravagant, too fabulous to include me. He gave the impression of never sleeping; his energy was more than manic; his partying—like his performances—took on mythic proportions. So I kept my distance. I'm not obsequious by nature and could never curry favor. But even when certain social opportunities presented themselves, I backed off. I feared rejection.

Yet those three months in *Golden Boy* during the summer of 1965 were significant. I saw myself rising to a new level of achievement. In spite of my faux pas, my confidence was renewed. I had, after all, played Broadway with Sammy Davis, Jr. In September, with the musical still going strong, fortune or fate or pure luck suddenly broke my way in the form of a familiar play. When a European impresario offered me the part of Sportin' Life in a *Porgy and Bess* originating in Vienna, my earlier ambivalence dissolved. I was ready.

Sammy was not happy about my leaving. I took his displeasure as a compliment. Ironically, I was leaving to assume a role which he had, in the eyes of many, immortalized.

"Bob's Sportin' Life was unique," said Karin, who saw me play the part in rehearsals before we left for Europe. "Sammy was fun-loving and charming. Bob infused the role with something darker, ominous, even threatening. His portrayal was deep."

In my mind, I was hired because of the dubious distinction of being able to sing the score note for note. The Austrians wanted a *Porgy* as it had been written by Gershwin. That meant minimum musical frills. There is, for instance, a key scene in which Sportin' Life tries to convince Bess to escape with him to New York. Others had played the scene broadly. I had my own view of Sportin' Life. I could never play him according to someone else's idea of a black man. I saw him as a straightforward character. I thought he had his own sense of worth. I didn't see him as a stereotype, and because I refused to ridicule him, I think he became more complex. I strove to make him real.

In 1965, the year I left for Vienna, Martin Luther King led three thousand protestors on a march from Selma to Montgomery, Alabama, original capital of the Confederacy. They brought to Governor George Wallace a petition demanding the right to vote and an end to police brutality. King was joined by twenty-five thousand sympathizers, among them Harry Belafonte, James Baldwin, Leonard Bernstein, and Peter, Paul and Mary. King spoke, and five months later Lyndon Johnson signed the Voting Rights Act into law.

In Europe, I regarded the movement's progress with quiet satisfaction. We were finally getting our due. Karin, who had put her heart and soul into the work, had even more reason to rejoice. I was also pleased that the political climate in America, combined with the attitude of the Viennese audience, allowed for a *Porgy and Bess* closer to my sensibility. We didn't have to spook it up. The focus was on musicality, not racial stereotypes. It was a pleasure to play the part without the bells and whistles often employed by American directors. In Europe those were seen as distractions from the score's basic beauty. Another bonus was the presence of William Warfield as Porgy, the same Warfield who had toured the world in the 1950s production with Leontyne Price.

I was a success. Theatergoers liked my portrayal, and for the next seven years I would return to Vienna to play the part forty-five days each spring and forty-five days each fall. That first fall, when I saw that my interpretation was well received, I was especially full of myself. My singing was true to Gershwin's melodies, and my dancing, while never extraordinary, incorporated enough natural movement to be convincing. Strong reviews and loud cheers emboldened me. I thought that perhaps one day soon I could carry a major show.

Jimmy Randolph, strikingly handsome and irresistibly gregarious, played Crown. Jimmy loved people. He was also a magnet for beautiful women. When I first arrived in Vienna, I rented a dismal one-room flat. Once it became clear, though, that the play was a success, Jimmy and I began sharing a suite at the Intercontinental Hotel. I was hoping Jimmy's way with women might work to my advantage. In the small world of Viennese theater, we were celebrities. As black men, we were also seen as exotic by certain Viennese females. Without equivocation, I sought sexual adventures. I found those willing women especially enticing in light of my less than enthusiastic view of the city and its male citizens. To a large degree, I found Vienna provincial and the Viennese cold. Their assumptions about American blacks irritated me. They complained about the prejudice of American political institutions even as they revealed their own prejudices. After a few drinks, I'd invariably hear them describe us as comically lazy or intellectually inferior. Arguing wasn't easy. It was more than a matter of my German, which, after a while, was fairly fluent. As debaters, the Austrians projected a formality that was difficult to penetrate. Another kind of penetration was of far greater interest to me. The presence of women eager to have sex was the one civic trait I came to cherish.

The impresario was a certain Marcel Prawy. At first I viewed Herr Prawy favorably. I thought him erudite and gracious. But I soon saw him differently. While mounting a production of *La Boheme,* he told a black singer, whose voice was magnificent, that she was simply "too ugly" to play the part of Mimi. She knew—as did I—that he was referring to the darkness of her skin. The cruelty of his remarks unhinged me. I saw him as a secret racist and grew to resent him, an awkward attitude to maintain since he was, after all, my boss. That didn't stop me from looking for ways to get under his skin. Before each performance, for example, he'd strut on stage and, in lofty German, announce the commencement of the greatest production of the greatest opera with the greatest cast assembled in the greatest opera house in all of Europe. When his little speech was over and he reached the wings, I'd invariably lean over and whisper in his ear, "Bullshit. This is a second-tier opera house and you know it. Besides, other casts have been better. Why do you keep feeding the audience bullshit?"

Why did I feel compelled to antagonize the man? Why did I view his promotional hype as anything but an impresario's right? Despite my success—or perhaps because of it—the rebel within me was spoiling for a fight. Part of me acknowledged the fact that this man was giving me yearly employment. Another part resented his power. I knew that it was the strength of my performance, not his love of Negroes, that kept me around. I also knew that he harbored an array of assumptions about blacks I found abhorrent. I was on to him, and I needed to let him know. My antagonism probably cost me roles in other plays he was producing. I was either too stupid, too headstrong, too immature, or too shortsighted to curb my caustic barbs. I remember sometime before a female friend had warned me about this very thing. She had watched me engage in a vitriolic exchange with another man. I've long forgotten the topic. As usual, I was unyielding. I pulled out every verbal weapon at my command. Only when my foe was thoroughly vanquished did I stop. "Isn't it funny, Robert," said my female friend, "how you always have to be right, no matter what?" My first reaction was to argue with her. But I couldn't. Arguing with her would have just proven her point.

Arguments with Karin became more commonplace. Women know when their men are wandering. My inability to see that her commitment to me required a commitment of my own played havoc with our relationship. It never dawned on me to divorce my wife and marry her, though she might have been waiting for me to ask. This was part of my continuing ignorance, or lack of consciousness. I lacked the emotional strength to give her my all.

"I was in the throes of all kinds of personal changes," Karin recalled. "I hated myself for being jealous. I saw jealousy as a middle-class emotion. And I saw marriage as a middle-class institution. I had always been antiestablishment. I was a beatnik in the fifties and now, in the sixties, I was quite the hippie. I'd always embraced aberrant behavior. Well, that was fine as sociological perspective, but when it came to my lover, aberrant behavior didn't cut it. I fought the feelings; I longed to be free of suspicions and doubts. But the truth was staring me in the face. Bob's a sexy man. Women adore him. He loved being adored—who doesn't?—and was a shameless flirt. He simply couldn't keep his hand out of the cookie jar."

Karin's view was to accept people as they are. For most of the sixties, she tried to do that with me. She worked on her writing. She published in alternative music magazines—*Rolling Stone* and *Cream*— and contributed a column to the *East Village Other.* Her passion for jazz had widened to include rock 'n' roll, especially the rebels like Dylan. She had a life outside of me.

"Bob's sons would visit us in the summertime," she said, "and I saw how much they loved him. Kevin, the oldest, looked like his mom; Jacques favored his dad. Bob took them to his shows and gave them a good taste of what the business is all about. It's no surprise that they both became musicians and entertainers. I have no doubt that Bob always wanted to do the right thing—by his kids and by me. Our intellectual rapport never diminished. Nor did the sexual excitement. That's why we stayed together as long as we did. And that's why it took me so goddamn long to cut it off. I wanted him, and I did all I could to look the other way. As he became successful, he became even more charming. He'd pick up foreign languages—French, German, Dutch, Italian—in a matter of weeks. He became worldlier, more sophisticated, and self-assured. All this added to his allure. I'd discover an affair of his, swear that was it, and then a week later find myself in bed with him, drawn to the same heat that neither of us could resist."

Karin had a capacity to love that I lacked. I don't say that lightly or offer it as an excuse. It's simply fact. My sense of self was rooted in my work. In the theater, I had finally found a place where I could be myself. As I looked back at my earlier life and long history of occupational unrest, I saw the cause of my discontent: I wanted to be free. I wanted to be free not only to pursue what I chose, but to conduct that pursuit on my own terms. Having a boss or being bossed was repugnant. To a large extent, theater allowed a latitude that felt like freedom. Yet even within that world I often found myself faced with an old enemy—authority. It was in the midsixties at the Arena Stage Theater in Washington, D. C., for example, that I was performing *Ballad for Americans,* a musical piece written by Earl Robinson and originally played by Paul Robeson. I had learned the songs well. I interpreted them with confidence and, I thought, understanding. The musical director disagreed. He suggested I give the lyrics a different reading. I resisted and, I was convinced, clearly stated my case. The director, however, had no interest in my case. After a few rehearsals in which I was less than compliant, he sent me packing. I was astounded. Even then, I still didn't get it. The firing haunted me for years. What the hell had I done wrong? Can't a man express an opinion without being shot down? I couldn't see what the director saw: that I was insufferably headstrong.

And it wasn't just singing, it was acting as well. I remember a fellow actor telling me that with my haughty attitude I'd never get anywhere. My rejoinder was, "Then why has your attitude of fawning compliance gotten you no further than me?" It took a woman to cut through my bull. Barbara Ann Teer, who founded the Black Theater Ensemble of Harlem, was a close friend. I greatly admired her work. She and I would often read scripts together. We might be preparing for an audition or just working on our technique. One evening when we were reading aloud, Barbara stopped me out of the blue and said, "I don't believe you. I don't believe a word you're saying." I was indignant. "What do you mean you don't believe me?" "You sound like you're acting," she said. "Damn it, Barbara," I barked, "that's the whole point." "That's not the point," she replied. "The point, Bob, is for the audience to believe you. You have to make us feel it." I tried to dismiss the idea. Surely I had projected sufficient feeling. My reading was perfectly reasonable. My execution was wholly professional. I cared nothing about this never-never land of make-believe emotions. I knew what I was doing; I employed professional techniques. Yet the more I thought about what Barbara had said, the more I realized she was right. I needed to go deeper. And yet emotional depth was the very thing I found so frightening. Addressing my fears, and including them in my work, was foreign to me. As the sixties grew more complex, as my life and career took new and unexpected turns, I kept hearing Barbara's words: "I don't believe you."

My grandmother, Jeannette Williams

My sister Cleo

My sister Dolores

St. Nicholas Elementary School. I'm the last child on the right on the first row.

My preteen look

My brother, James

The army, 1945

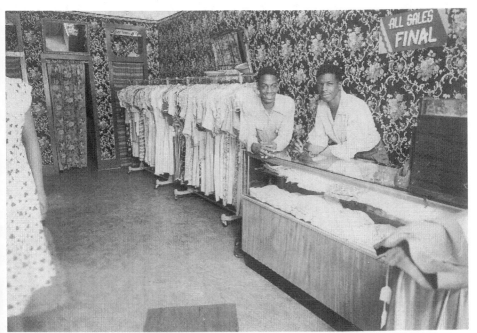

The Geraldine Shoppe, St. Louis, 1950. Jack LaZard is on the right.

Karin Berg, at 23, in Cleveland during the late 1950s

# Robert Guillaume

## TENOR

### Recent Engagements

**BROADWAY**
Tambourines to Glory
Kwamina
Fly Blackbird
Katherine Dunham's
"Bamboche"

**WORLD TOUR**
Free and Easy

**CONCERT TOUR**
Bob DeCormier Singers

**TELEVISION**
Tonight Show
The Gershwin Years

The remarkable variety of Robert Guillaume's program is matched by his own career. Born and raised in St. Louis, he worked at many jobs, including streetcar-motorman, mailman and candy-maker, before he completed his musical and academic education at St. Louis University. His musical career began in 1958 when he joined the famed Karamu Players in Cleveland, appearing in many productions from musical comedy to opera. In 1959 he came to New York and was immediately cast in the world tour of "Free and Easy." Since his return in 1960 he has played featured roles in a number of Broadway shows, has made several network TV appearances, has gone on national concert tours, has worked nightclubs, coffee houses and Israeli Cafes and has made many individual appearances at luncheons, community centers and resort hotels. His repertoire includes showtunes, folksongs in many languages, spirituals and arias. To all these songs he brings a wide variety of mood and style as well as a thrilling tenor voice, making him one of the most exciting and talked about young artists in the entertainment field.

## What the Critics Say

**TAMBOURINES TO GLORY**
"Robert Guillaume provides its most attractive number as he sings ever so easily a ballad called 'Moon Outside My Window.'" Walter Kerr, Herald Tribune
"A lovely ballad 'Moon Outside My Window' was magnificently sung by Mr. Guillaume." John McClain, Journal American
"Robert Guillaume has the best leading man voice on Broadway and there is no argument about that and I trust the disc-makers have the wit to engage him to record 'Moon Outside My Window.'" Whitney Bolton, Morning Telegraph

**KWAMINA**
"The best number in the show 'Nothing More to Look Forward to' sung by Ethel Ayler and Bob Guillaume." Walter Kerr, Herald Tribune
"Any score that includes as lovely a song as 'Nothing More to Look Forward to' sung with tender expressiveness by Robert Guillaume and Ethel Ayler should not be allowed to drift off to the limbo of forgotten musicals." John Wilson, Sunday Times

**FLY BLACKBIRD**
"Robert Guillaume sings with irresistible vitality." Howard Taubman, N. Y. Times

My promo sheet, the early 1960s

The Pilgrims (l to r): myself, Angeline Butler, and Gilbert Price, 1965

As Sportin' Life in *Porgy and Bess,* Vienna, the mid-1960s

The cast of *Jacques Brel*, 1968

With Ron O'Neal during *Superfly T.N.T.*, Rome, 1973

Dancing with Faye Hauser at a party for *Guys and Dolls,* 1977

The cast of *Soap*, ABC–TV, 1977

The cast of *Benson*, ABC–TV, 1979

My first Emmy, 1979

My sons (from left): Jacques and Kevin, the mid-1980s

Jacques and Marlene

My daughters (l to r): Rachel, Pat, Melissa

Jacques

Donna Brown Guillaume

*Phantom of the Opera,* 1990

*Sports Night*, ABC–TV, 1998, photo by Bob D'Amico

The family today: Rachel and Donna

# Pilgrims' Progress

The "Pilgrims" wasn't a bad name. It was catchy enough. It contained a certain irony that worked in the context of the sixties when vocal groups—think of the Beatles and Byrds—bore little resemblance to their namesakes. I liked the notion of being a Pilgrim, even without being certain of its musical connotation. What I liked even more was the possibility of a big commercial success. If that meant being a Pilgrim, so be it.

The idea for the group was cooked up by my friend Tom Wilson. Tom was a brilliant brother from Texas who became close to both Karin and me. We hung out in Village folk clubs and jazz spots, where we discussed and resolved all world problems. Tom was a Harvard man who, at six feet six, was an imposing figure and a towering intellect. His worked as an artists and repertoire executive for Columbia Records, where he had supervised Bob Dylan and Simon and Garfunkel. It was Tom's innovative studio work that shaped the sound of "Like a Rolling Stone" and "The Sounds of Silence." When we met Tom, he was on a roll.

Tom liked my voice. Having heard me at a club singing a mix of Broadway ballads, Israeli folk songs, and Neapolitan arias, he approached me about recording. Naturally I was game. I envisioned a solo effort. But Tom had something else in mind. At the time, Peter, Paul and Mary were red hot. Hits like "Blowin' in the Wind" and "Puff, the Magic Dragon" had topped the charts. The image of folk artists-gone-pop struck the right chord in the left-leaning sixties. Before rock got rough, Peter, Paul and Mary had a lilting sound and an attractive look that worked commercial wonders. Tom sought to replicate their appeal by a forming a trio of black singers—two men and a woman—whose repertoire consisted of similar folk-pop. It wasn't the solo shot I was hoping for, but it was better than pounding the pavement. With Tom at the helm, I had high hopes.

He called us the Pilgrims—myself, Angeline Butler, and Gilbert Price. Angeline and Gilbert had superb voices, and the material, while soft, was just what the doctor ordered. We cut a record for Columbia. Thanks to Tom, the label laid it all out for us: Richard Avedon shot a fashion photo of us with Louis Armstrong for *Vogue.* We were booked into hip clubs like the Cellar in Washington, D. C. We created a stir. Yet in spite of bright prospects, the group collapsed. The cause was internal dissension, which, I'm afraid, had much to do with me. Angeline and I did not get along. Like Karin, Angeline had been a Freedom Rider. She was smart and self-assured. She had her opinions. I had mine. Whether it was song selection or wardrobe choices, we agreed on practically nothing. We were both unyielding. After awhile, we tired of each other's intransigence. I blamed it on her high sense of herself; she blamed it on my unrestrained ego. Either way, our ersatz group reached an impasse. If we had enjoyed a smash record, we might have been more motivated to get along. But that never happened. Instead, the trio quickly dissolved, and we returned to our former lives, Pilgrims no more.

My friendship with Tom survived the debacle. In a few years I would find that the Pilgrim experience had served me well. My musical repertoire had expanded, and I was more likely to tackle projects outside my prescribed genres. Still, I wish I had been less obstreperous with Angeline. I wish that part of me which delighted in disputation could, once and for all, just shut up. But maturation came slowly, if at all, and I remained prisoner of a temperament I was not interested in understanding. Besides, there was always the escape to Europe, twice a year, year after year, that let me lick my wounds and regain my footing. Sportin' Life had a long life.

The life I left behind in St. Louis was forgotten but for my sons. I loved them dearly, sent money when I could, brought them to New

York when possible. I had little contact with my mother, brother, and sisters. I still maintained great emotional distance between myself and my childhood. But my children were another matter. My absenteeism was nothing I could ignore. I was guilty and, even more, sorely missed the boys. So in 1966, when *Porgy and Bess* was booked to play Israel over the summer, I arranged for Kevin and Jacques to sing in the chorus.

"I was always glad to hear from Bob," Marlene remembered, "although months might pass without a word. I worked at a hospital, my grandmother worked as a domestic, and we somehow muddled through. I never bad-mouthed Bob to the boys. It pained me to constantly be looking to him for support, but I had little choice. I always felt that he could do better, just as he always felt he was doing his best. Our emotional relationship had ended years before. Now it was just about money. Our living conditions were always very plain, and month-to-month sustenance was a concern. When Bob called to say he was actually taking the boys for a full summer, everyone was thrilled. The boys longed to spend time with their dad—not just a quick visit to New York, but an extended period of actually living with him. Kevin especially adored Bob. Jacques had feelings about how his father had left us, but once he learned he was going abroad, he could hardly sleep. It was a good thing for everyone."

Kevin has vivid memories of the trip: "I was ten, Jacques was eight, and we were giddy with joy. We'd never been on a plane, and suddenly we're with Pops flying over the ocean to a country where Jesus walked on water. We were sheltered little Catholic schoolboys, who instantly became heroes when our schoolmates learned where we were going. It was the most exciting thing that had ever happened to us. It changed our lives. The truth is, I'll still be thinking of the trip in my afterlife. Not only were we exposed to all the history and beauty of Israel, we were part of a big colorful theatrical production. We were kids in the Catfish Row community of *Porgy and Bess,* on stage, singing, dressed up in costumes, bathed in gels and spotlights, surrounded by the sounds of a full orchestra, facing an audience of cheering adults.

We went to bed every night past midnight. During the days, we'd explore ancient cities, float in the Dead Sea, swim in the Mediterranean, visit Mount Sinai. It was unreal. And so were the evenings when we entered the make-believe world of the theater, putting on makeup and pretending we were street urchins in Charleston, South Carolina. For both me and Jacques, the greasepaint got under our skin—and stayed there forever."

The tour was under the auspices of the Habimah National Theater of Israel. Val Pringle played Crown, and I resumed the role of Sportin' Life. We performed all over the country—in Jaffa, Haifa, in kibbutzim in the desert and in villages by the sea. Our longest stay was in Tel Aviv, where I found a three-bedroom apartment in a pleasant section of the city called Ramat Gian. It was an idyllic time.

Back in Vienna, I'd been involved with an Englishwoman, and she, along with her little girl from her former marriage, accompanied me and the boys. We became a makeshift family of five. Given the extreme exotic setting, it was easy to convince myself that I was in love. I certainly loved being around my sons, and my feeling for this woman was unusually strong. Just as strong were my feelings for Israel. I was comfortable in a country that seemed to harbor no prejudice toward American blacks. I relished the sky and sea and sun, the relaxed ambience of the restaurants and open-air bars, the savory food, the layer upon layer of archeological ruins, the sound of an ancient language reborn, and the sense of a people for whom culture—music, literature, theater—is paramount.

I was delighted to see my children's natural affinity for the stage. They were little stars, singing brightly, dancing smartly, following directions like old pros. The cast adored them. They were also little hams. One night, at Val Pringle's suggestion, as a prank Kevin stepped out and took an individual bow. The audience howled. Afterward, it was my duty to tell the kid he was out of line. Jacques was also an extrovert. Cast as the son of Serena, the woman who sings "My Man's Gone Now," he had learned her part so well that he'd sing the words sotto voce while she belted out the famous aria. One evening, when the regular Serena fell ill and her understudy stepped in, Jacques was no longer sotto voce. In an attempt to help the understudy, Jacques sang almost as loudly as she. His little-boy voice was impressive, though later I pointed out the inappropriateness of his well-meaning gesture.

The Israelis treated me marvelously. They made me feel like a celebrity. The women were particularly alluring—easy to talk to, vigorous, sinuous, smart, and sexually liberal. My own sexuality, a dominant force in my life, was thrown into overdrive. I fell for a nineteen-year-old beauty. The affair was really an affair within an affair since my English girlfriend and I were in the midst of an affair. Perhaps the multiple levels of intrigue fueled my fires. Or perhaps, more simply, I was a deceitful son-of-a-bitch drawn to the thrill of seduction. In the case of the Israeli, there was the added component of danger. She was the daughter of ultra-Orthodox Jews and lived in a section of Tel Aviv where had we been caught together, we might have been stoned. She enjoyed smashing the cultural taboos as much as I did. Whatever the reasons, the sex was sensational.

At summer's end, I put my sons on a plane back to St. Louis. I was moving on to Toulouse with *Porgy*. For a flash, I thought about keeping the boys—having them stay with me in Europe, then live with me in New York. I told myself, though, that that would be unfair; I'd be uprooting them and breaking their mother's heart. Ultimately, however, my failure to spend more time with my sons stemmed not from consideration for Marlene but from my ongoing insensitivity.

"Jacques and I flew home alone," Kevin remembered, "knowing nothing would ever be the same. We were little men. The trip had changed us. For the first time in our lives, we had really bonded with Pops. I was in awe of him. To see my father command a stage and bring people to their feet made a mighty impression on my ten-year-old mind. That was the summer when Jacques and I fell in love with show business. We'd visit Pops in New York every summer for the rest of our childhoods. But it was our time in Israel that made the difference. Dad made us feel part of his world. And that world, filled with music and magic, was the one we wanted, the one we'd remember all winter long. We missed our mother and we loved her dearly. We knew she'd devoted her life to us. But now we knew our father was a star, and our heads were filled with dreams."

Europe provided steady work. *Porgy* played in Bregenz, Austria, where they built a stage in front of an authentic Mississippi steamboat moored on a mountain lake. There a famous composer said to me, at a party after the performance, "My dear Robert, I haven't seen hips like yours since the sixteenth century." I accepted the compliment without quite understanding it and moved on. In France, a leading retailer liked my looks and invited me to be photographed, dressing me in wools and worsteds and smartly tailored camel hair coats. My love of fine clothes, not to mention my vanity, nearly had me heading to Paris; this woman was certain I'd clean up as a fashion model. Regaining my good sense, I thanked her for the lovely pictures and declined. Anne Brown, who had played the original Bess in 1935, was asked to direct another *Porgy* in Norway and wanted me and my Sportin' Life to come along. I considered the offer. I even considered giving up New York and making Europe my permanent residence. There was a certain sense to that. Black artists, starving in the States, have often thrived in Europe. The lifestyle is attractive. Europeans are adept at making American blacks feel special. I thought of James Baldwin and jazz musician Dexter Gordon. I knew many black expatriates; I understood the attraction of abandoning home once and for all. But with that abandonment comes certain pain. Expatriation was an estrangement from one's roots too extreme even for me. I had to get back to New York. I had done well in Europe, but I had not really made it in the place that, for better or worse, had defined me—those troubled United States.

# "He Had Specters . . ."

"Bob's specters," Karin observed, "were hard to define. Like all ghosts, they were formless. But I know they pursued him, even haunted him. They had to do with pain. I'd guess they went back to his mother and all the wounds of childhood. Bob hid those wounds. He was hard to read. Emotional introspection was not his style. Therapy wasn't even a remote possibility, and, as probing as our intellectual conversations may have been, certain personal areas were off-limits. In many ways, Bob had broken free of his background. But in other ways, he had not. The idea of talking to a psychologist, a perfect stranger, about intimate issues was anathema to him. Rather than process those feelings, he stuffed them. And there wasn't much I, or anyone, could do about it."

Karin and I had lived together for six or seven years. Cohabitation had taken its toll. So had our insular lifestyle. We invited over only extremely close friends, and we never gave parties. Our relationship, while not secret, was far from public. No matter, she had made the adjustment and would have gone on had it not been for my outside relationships. There were just too many affairs to ignore. Reacting to them, she had the odd affair herself but told me they were never satisfying. She said she just wanted me. I wanted to be left alone to do as I pleased. Our clashes increased—I was up late; she was up early; I was reading for a play; she was writing an article; when I was working she wanted my attention and vice versa. When all the white workers of CORE were kicked out in 1968, Karin was depressed. I said, "Karin, you'll find another organization and another reason to ignore me." For all her attention, I continued to feel a strange loneliness, a loneliness that, according to Karin, resided deep within me.

Despite our growing problems, I supported Karin's writing and was proud when she started publishing on a regular basis. As she started her lateral move from music journalism to the music business itself, she grew more independent. Eventually she wound up working for David Geffen. She was head of publicity for Elektra/Asylum and, over the next decades, brought in several key groups to major labels. These were all talents she genuinely admired. Her work became more significant. She realized she had an ear and a point of view to offer the industry. When the industry was receptive, her sense of achievement was high. As her career took shape, she realized that her happiness wasn't dependent upon me.

"For all our great talks and great sex," Karin said, "I was miserable being with a man incapable of real commitment. His long absences compounded our problems. So, after months of heartache, we decided to live apart. I knew I was doing the right thing, but that didn't stop me from crying uncontrollably. Bob found a place in Lincoln Towers and I stayed put. But that didn't stop us from seeing each other and often sleeping together. It took years for us to call it off entirely—that's how strongly we were drawn to one another. Our pattern of make up and break up seemed endless. Once in the late sixties, just back from Vienna, Bob suggested we live together again. I was tempted, but by then I knew better. An occasional reunion was one thing, but not a shared home. I loved him, but I didn't trust him."

I understood lust far more than love. I was not good at love; I'm not even sure I understood the emotion. If anything, I felt that, as a boy, I had been humiliated by love. A boy loves his mother, and when his mother is indifferent, when love is rebuffed, love is not to be trusted. At a relatively early age, I recall telling myself that I would never love anyone. As ridiculous as that sounds, that silent mantra echoed inside my head, even as I approached forty. When I returned to New York, I did not feel guilty because of the women I had enjoyed in Europe. I'm not sure I felt anything. I was grateful to Karin for her support and belief in me—she had been in my corner for more than a decade—but I was incorrigible. I failed to realize the gravity, failed to see that loyalty demands loyalty. I had built a wall around myself. And while that meant no one—not even Karin—could get in, it also meant I could never get out.

We're all looking for breakthroughs. I know I was—not a personal, but a professional, breakthrough. Actors survive on hopes and dreams, and the biggest dream is that one role will catapult you to fortune and fame. My progress as an artist was far more important to me than my development as a person. The frustrating thing, of course, was my inability to control that progress. A career in acting is a study in frustration. You go to readings; you join small theater companies and take nonpaying parts; you find workshops and teachers. But mostly you audition and wait. You listen for the phone. You wait for a call that, in a matter of seconds, will transform your life from the mundane to magical. I watched my Karamu friend Ron O'Neal go through a magical transition and, despite a twinge of envy, celebrated his triumph.

In the late sixties, Ron starred in Charles Gordone's *No Place to Be Somebody*. Drama critic Walter Kerr called Gordone "the most astonishing new American playwright to come along since Edward Albee." Gordone appreciated the designation. A black man, he did not consider himself part of the black theater movement, although he lamented how, in his words, "the commercial theater—the Broadway stage—depicts blacks in sensational and stereotypical ways without showing any interest in the black experience." His play was a brilliant depiction of the black experience—he called it a "black black comedy"—a tour de force that won the Pulitzer Prize. For Ron, who had grown up with Chuck in Cleveland, it was a career-altering experience. In the lead role, he brought the drama to life, winning an Obie (an off-Broadway Tony) in the process. Ron was suddenly the darling of New York critics, the right actor in the right play at the right time. In short order, Ron would parlay the success into the film persona Superfly. Gordone would fall into obscurity and wind up teaching at Texas A&M. He was an iconoclast who never toed the line of political correctness among blacks, eschewing traditional organizations and causes. His legacy was this one great play.

While Ron's breakthrough was major, mine was minor. It came about through a part in an obscure musical revue by an obscure songwriter. The part did not call for a black man. I liked that. I liked that I was the only black member of a cast that had originally been conceived as all white. I'm speaking of *Jacques Brel Is Alive and Well and Living in Paris,* a piece that pushed my career in a new direction.

Mort Shuman instigated the endeavor. Along with his former partner, Doc Pomus, Shuman had written many hits, including "Viva Las Vegas" for Elvis and "This Magic Moment" for the Drifters. Then while visiting Paris, Shuman discovered the songs of Brel, a contemporary poet-singer from Belgium some called the European Bob Dylan. Now collaborating with Eric Blau, Shuman translated and adapted Brel's compositions into a revue that opened at the Village Gate, an upstairs/downstairs jazz club. The cast consisted of four vocalists, and they performed twenty-five songs. It was, in essence, the first librettoless musical. The translations were superb and sang like poetry. Brel had made a name for himself in the French cabaret style. If he'd been born earlier, he might have been a protégé of Edith Piaf's. He was a vehemently antibourgeoisie populist who viewed humanity with bittersweet bias. There was a touch of cynicism in Brel's work that I found sympathetic.

I was called to audition at the Village Gate. Shuman himself was in the original cast and needed an understudy. A few nights later, Morty's voice gave out and I stepped in. It was tricky. The material was complex and the staging fast-paced. I barely avoided bumping into furniture and other singers. I barely remembered the lyrics. At the close of the first act, I sang "Amsterdam," a powerful profile of a city. The song builds to a dramatic crescendo. When I was through, there was a hush—a disconcertingly long hush—followed by a roar so damn loud I jumped. The roar, it turned out, was for me. I was in.

What began as a small cult hit slowly evolved into an international sensation. Off and on, I played the show for four years. Thirty-three years later, *Jacques Brel Is Alive and Well and Living in Paris* is still being performed. Born in the midst of anti-Vietnam sentiment, the revue hit the right emotional chord. Beyond its antiestablishment sentiments, *Brel* spoke to people on a basic emotional level. I was proud to be in the company. I saw it as a coup, precisely the kind of barrier-breaking part I'd been seeking. These were not stereotypical characterizations. I could be who I wanted to be—a free black man. The individuality inherent in Brel's songs elicited the individuality within me. For the first time, I could stand on stage and not give a damn whether the audience liked me or not. The music was defiant, and so was I. Ironically, the more defiant, the more effective my delivery. Not all my black partners understood. "Bob," they said after seeing my performance, "you look mad. You don't smile. The audience will think you've got an attitude." Well, I did. And so did Brel. The songs were idiosyncratic. A woman sang about the love of two gay men, one of whom was dying. "We'll dance across the moon," she quotes one of the lovers. "Turn midnight into noon, pour perfume on the breezes . . . I'll squeeze out all the tears, the newsreel of our life I'll play it in reverse." We sang a song called "The Desperate Ones," evoking a scene of lost love that left the audience in tears. The sparseness of the show—the simplicity of costume and single piano accompaniment—highlighted the haunting melodies. Our Israeli director and choreographer, Moni Yakim, understood movement and mood. It was a mordant revue, a penetrating look into the hearts and souls of *Brel's* cast of disparate characters.

The venue's intimacy added to the allure. The patrons at the Gate were on top of us, and the emotional exchange especially powerful. I had been singing since I was a boy, but never—not in church, not in my classical recitals, not in *Kwamina* or *Blackbird* or *Porgy*—had I truly realized my ability to disarm an audience. Because I was armed with such strong stories, *Brel* awakened my consciousness as a musical actor.

Gigging at the Gate had unique side benefits. While we performed upstairs, a dazzling array of artists were downstairs. These were the golden years of Nina Simone, for whom the Gate was a second home. Lit by a single spot, seated at the grand piano, she cut a striking figure, elegant and proud. Night after night I'd wait for her to sing "Mississippi Goddamn." "Everybody knows about Mississippi goddamn," she'd bellow as the audience went wild. I've never seen protest rendered so dramatically. The Gate booked wonderful jazz musicians— Junior Mance, Cannonball Adderley, Sonny Rollins—as well as R&B acts like Junior Walker and flamenco dancers like Carmen Amaya.

As *Brel* caught on, the producers booked the revue in other cities, creating a number of touring companies. I was performing it in New York when the Arena Stage in Washington, D. C., offered me the role of Edmund in *King Lear.* I was tempted. I had long loved that dark play and was excited by the challenge. At the same time, I was asked to play *Brel* in Chicago, where prospects for a long-term run looked good. Coincidentally, Marlene had contacted me about our son Kevin. At twelve he was exhibiting some of the characteristics I knew all too well from my own adolescence. The teachers couldn't control him, and neither could his mother. Would I be willing to let him live with me? Faced with that decision, I saw that Chicago was the place to go.

"I couldn't wait to get to Chicago," Kevin remembered. "I was into my full-tilt rebellion, and I needed—and wanted—to have a father, rather than a mother, in charge. Pops put me in a Catholic school, no surprise since that's the kind of training I'd been used to, and the only kind I really trusted. We lived at the Churchill Hotel, across the street from the Ambassador East, in a swanky part of town. Chicago was cool but crazy. This was the year of the infamous Democratic convention when cops were attacking protestors and the city went wild. I didn't mind. I liked the excitement. Anything was better than St. Louis. Besides, sometimes Dad would take me out to hear Oscar Peterson at the London House or Richard Pryor at Mister Kelly's. I loved it all. My cultural education was expanding and my school behavior improving. I was just plain happy being around show business. As a kid, I'd agonized over my folks not being together. I never found a way to reconcile the fact that both my parents were nice people who had nothing to do with each other. The polarity was always there. Instinctually, I sided with Pops. Jacques was made to resent Pops, not by our mother, who always spoke well of him, but by Mom's family, who never forgave him for skipping out."

Diahann Carroll had the title role in *Julia*, a pioneering situation comedy that premiered on network television in 1968. I was performing *Jacques Brel* in Los Angeles that year when *Julia*'s producer, Hal Kantor, saw the show and asked me to make a guest appearance. I was pleased. Any sort of decent acting work would have pleased me, but television was particularly interesting because I had never done it before. Additionally, *Julia* was an important show; for the first time, a black single mother was depicted as a heroine. The situation was thoroughly middle class, in a positive sense: Julia was a nurse raising a son. Diahann was a luminous beauty who played the part with great aplomb. In my single appearance, I was cast as a car salesman. Strictly speaking, the show was a comedy. I saw that the camera picked up the smallest movement, the slightest expression, so minimalism made sense. In comedy, timing is all. And in that regard, my model was Buster Keaton, who let his face speak while his mouth stayed silent. I went to the soundstage in Hollywood and played my few scenes with some facility. The director was not displeased. I considered the power of the medium. A day's worth of TV work paid more than a month's work on the stage. On stage you're seen by hundreds; on TV, millions. Who wouldn't be impressed? I didn't fantasize about a career in television because it seemed neither logical nor likely. I had not the smallest instinct that the medium held my future. I simply reasoned that a TV gig now and then might be sweet. There was effort involved, to be sure, but nothing like singing twenty-six songs over the course of a night. And while my friends in the New York theater might look down on the boob tube, it seemed like things were improving. In the light of the civil rights movement, popular culture was in flux. *Beulah* and *Amos and Andy* were long lost in the fog of the distant fifties. Diahann Carroll, her dignity intact, could command her own show. And she could do so by portraying not a cook or maid, but a trained professional entering the American mainstream.

As the sixties gave way to the seventies, there was reason for optimism. I harbored high hopes of finding not just acting work but roles that transcended stereotypes. I found work, and the fact that my most important new role was, at its heart, stereotypical, carried unforeseen irony. In a career where I viewed race as incidental, race was becoming increasingly germane—and there wasn't a thing I could do about it.

# The Primary Issue

"Race is not merely an important issue," James Baldwin once said, "it is the primary issue that tests our morality as Americans." On another occasion Baldwin wrote, "I left America because I doubted my ability to survive the fury of the color problem here. . . . I wanted to prevent myself from becoming *merely* a Negro; or, even, merely a Negro writer. I wanted to find out in what way the *specialness* of my experience could be made to connect me with other people instead of dividing me from them." I related to Baldwin's assertions. I didn't want to be *merely* a black actor or black singer. I sought to define my own elusive *specialness*. My acting, like my singing, fell between the cracks. I was neither Sammy Davis nor Ezio Pinza. My musicality, like my theatricality, was hard to pinpoint. I wasn't obviously anything. I'd like to say I sought serious roles, but the truth is that, first and foremost, I sought roles. The seventies were a strange time for black actors.

"Ron O'Neal and Bob were best friends," remembered Carol Tillery Banks, a close friend of mine. "I met Ron in Cleveland, we married, and moved to a place off Central Park not far from Bob, who was living on West End Avenue. We became The Three Musketeers. The seventies had just kicked off, and it was fascinating to watch these two, so alike and yet so different, forge their careers. They were both hugely ambitious, highly intelligent, extremely gifted, and fiercely competitive. Not to mention handsome. They both bore the kind of anger black men of their backgrounds can't avoid. I respected their struggle to balance that anger with their drive to make it. These guys had come out of the neighborhood with a hunger for stardom. They'd achieve it, but the effects of stardom on their lives couldn't be more different. Bob's fame came slower and for that reason lasted longer. Ron's exploded. Part of Bob's armor was to intellectualize things, to reason his way down the tricky road of show business. I see him as a radical conservative—radical in thought but conservative in action. Ron was just plain radical. He lacked Bob's self-discipline. But he had the kind of bravura that made him Superfly. As serious-minded brothers, Ron and Bob were seeking their own personal dignities; that's what they brought to each character they played; and that's what was most inherent to their own character."

Thirty years later, the character of Superfly lives on, a permanent part of pop culture. The 1971 film, along with *Shaft*, is the classic by which all other works in the "blaxploitation" genre are measured. That genre of inner-city crime stories featuring all-black casts and bristling rhythm and blues scores is much loved and also much maligned. While there were certainly spurious films created in that mode, I saw *Superfly* as a singular achievement. I thought the movie had heart, and Ron, as the supersmooth ghetto operator, infused the character with complex electricity not to mention unflappable cool. Ron knew a host of superflys from his childhood in Cleveland. He respected their style, their smarts, and, of course, their way with women. He didn't judge them. He sought to immortalize them—and did just that. Ron's extraordinary look—most knew he was black, but many saw him as Latino or even Middle Eastern—added to the mystery. With his flowing locks, tall lean fame, and ghetto-fabulous wardrobe, Superfly became a hero—which is what got him in trouble with the black bourgeoisie.

Those haughty protectors of middle-class morality didn't like that Superfly snorted cocaine. They saw him celebrating a drug-driven lifestyle. Drugs have never interested me, and I don't condone them, but neither did Superfly. He wasn't celebrating the high life as much as he was struggling with its pitfalls. Superfly was looking to get out of the life, not go further into it. The fact that profits from the film went through the roof only muddled matters. Success is a bitch; chasing it or achieving it, you catch hell. Critics lauded Gordon Parks Jr.'s realistic direction; Curtis Mayfield's score deservedly won praise from all quarters; but Ron's instant superstar status rubbed critics—especially black intellectuals—the wrong way. Not only did they confuse Ron with his film persona, they were convinced he was giving the community a negative image; in short, we were looking bad in front of white folks. Three decades later, with the advent of gangsta rap, Superfly looks practically wholesome. But in the afterglow of the civil rights movement, when propriety and appearance still held sway, he was anathema to many. I recall attending a function at which a well-known black thespian excoriated Superfly. I took offense and took up Ron's case—as if he really needed me to do so. I was probably too caustic and failed to win any converts. Arguments hardly mattered: Superfly gave Ron the financial security and artistic autonomy we'd all been looking for. Meanwhile, I found myself playing the part of a Baptist preacher.

*Purlie* is the musical of Ossie Davis's play *Purlie Victorious.* Ossie wrote the book, and Gary Geld composed the rousing score. In 1970, it won a Tony. The lead role—preacherman Purlie—is a tour de force originally played magnificently by Cleavon Little. At the end of a profitable Broadway run, I took Cleavon's place. In 1971, I did the final two weeks in New York before going out on several national tours over a span of four years. *Purlie* became a significant event in my career. I carried the show to major cities across the country.

Ossie Davis, a black man, wrote his story with a satirical edge. His characters are archetypal by necessity; he was poking fun at old stereotypes. In a comedic sense, he was riffing on race relations. Some blacks took offense and found the piece condescending. I thought it was funny. I also thought that Cleavon Little, a son of the South, was well suited to the role. I was not. I was successful because the largely white audience didn't know the nuances of a real-life black preacher. I was operating on the principle that I could talk loud and long. But blacks who belonged to these churches knew I was a fraud. I felt their disappointment in my portrayal, yet there was little I could do. The script had sufficient humor, and the spirit of the production was positive. Purlie Victorious Judson is a self-ordained preacher who returns to his childhood home to buy back his church. He schemes to gain an inheritance and matches wits with a white bigot. Because Cleavon was not a singer, Purlie was given only one insignificant musical number. I was disappointed not to sing more, but the role's verbal demands kept me on my toes. I did it because it was there to do. It brought in money, kept my face in front of an audience, and entertained large groups of people.

The line between satirizing and stereotyping is thin. That whites support plays about blacks that many blacks find offensive is a troublesome phenomenon. *Porgy and Bess* was one such play, and, to a degree, so was *Purlie*. That I would prosper in two such productions speaks more to my notion of professionalism than artistic autonomy. I saw it this way: the purely professional works; the pure artist starves. I had no romantic illusions about starvation. I was going to avoid it at all costs. At the same time, I saw how other ethnic groups had somehow shed their cruder comic personas by entering the mainstream. Jews, for example, had kept the inflections of the Yiddish language but opted for standard English. The greatest of the Jewish comics—Milton Berle, Jack Benny, George Burns—dropped the Old World accents of their parents. On the other hand, the speech pattern of blacks has been used time and again—by black writers as well as whites—as a device for creating character. That can be illuminating, but also insulting. Negotiating the divide between healthy humor and condescension is tricky. Playing Purlie was tricky. My job was to make him funny. I did that, as was my custom, by playing him straight; I let the humor come out of the lines.

*Purlie* was tougher than *Jacques Brel*. *Brel* helped refine my sense of self. Race didn't enter the picture. But the picture changed radically when I found myself stepping into the shoes of a character with whom I had no natural rapport. "That's what acting is all about," said a friend when I expressed my insecurities. I overcame those insecurities but not the feeling of being misunderstood by my own people. I was not highly prized in the black community. Black theatergoers didn't know what to make of me. In my mind, I heard them asking themselves—What the heck is this guy up to? I keenly felt their disapproval, and because I lacked an ingratiating personality, there was nothing to do. I was a loner. I went my own way.

When the musical arrived in St. Louis, I was especially uncomfortable. Here, after all, were the city and family I had abandoned. I wanted to assume the role of local-boy-made-good, but my feelings were far from triumphant. My brother, James, came to see me, and his wife, Leona, helped sell large blocks of tickets to civic organizations. Dolores came and so did Cleo, who showed signs of the same suffering my mother had endured. She was hooked on drugs. My mother, who was still alive, might have attended, but I don't recall. I don't recall much of the play's run in St. Louis. Marlene, Kevin, and Jacques surely were there, but even their presence is a vague memory. This might have been the first time my sons met my sisters and their children. I wish I could report that I was able to fashion a family reunification, that old hurts were healed, and all lived happily ever after. The truth is that when I left St. Louis in the late fifties, I left with a vengeance. I made no attempt to keep up with my relatives, with the exception of my sons. I sealed myself off from my past. Returning made me uneasy. I had to face a broken family and the fact that I caused that break.

Old friends and acquaintances attended; the newspaper played up my St. Louis origins, and memories were jogged. On off days, I walked through the neighborhood of my childhood, now largely destroyed by urban renewal. Everyone was gone. I visited the campuses of St. Louis and Washington Universities, thinking of those tough-minded Jesuits and my teacher Leslie Chabay. My memories brought some glimmers of pleasure, but mainly there was pain. I walked through this landscape more attentive to the physical changes in the city than any psychological changes in me. I simply did not want to deal with the remnants of my earlier life.

For all my reservations about the role, *Purlie* brought me good fortune, particularly in the form of a female member of the cast. I was arrested by her beauty. Her personality was like honey; her mind was scintillating. I pursued her, and I caught her, and I found myself falling deep into a relationship that would ultimately test my mettle.

# Faye Hauser

"I grew up in Winston-Salem, North Carolina, where my own father was a highly respected member of the state legislature. In 1947, a decade before Rosa Parks, he refused to give up his seat on a segregated Greyhound bus. Political activism was a part of my upbringing. My parents encouraged independent thought and intellectual curiosity. I graduated from the University of North Carolina, majoring in drama and psychology, and moved to New York with the hope of acting, singing, and writing. I did all three.

"I met Bob in New York in 1973 during tryouts for a road company of *Purlie*. He was forty-six, I was in my twenties. At the time he was going with another woman, but his interest in me was clear. I was flattered. Who wouldn't be? Bob was engaging and handsome, a wonderful conversationalist, dapper dresser, and, most impressive to all of us in the cast, the star of the show. I'd known pseudosophisticates, but there was nothing pseudo about Bob. His sophistication was based upon years of theatrical experience, both here and abroad. When I got in the show and found myself on tour—performing in Miami, Philadelphia, and Los Angeles—Bob's attention was irresistible. I was especially vulnerable, coming off a difficult relationship where my heart had been broken. My ex-boyfriend had proven quite crazy. Bob was anything *but* crazy. He seemed—and was—completely stable. A few friends warned of the dangers of a May-December affair, but I wasn't listening. I was too busy falling in love. And besides, the quality of Bob's character was a given. Everyone respected him. I admired his commitment to his sons; he cared for them deeply. He was different from the theater people I had known. Less flashy. More sincere. Certainly more serious. He had a wonderful combination of sexiness and stability. He was a man who knew the ways of the world and seemed, at least on the surface, comfortable with those ways. Occasionally I saw signs of his discomfort and indications of his troubled past. We might be walking in the city, for example, and passing by St. Patrick's Cathedral. I loved to go inside, just to meditate upon the grandeur of the sanctuary and beauty of the art. But Bob would freeze up and refuse to enter. His refusal had everything to do with the mystery of his childhood, an area he refused to discuss."

Before I came along, Faye was minding her own business, rehearsing the show, doing well. She possessed enormous talent and beauty. Early on, I saw she had star quality; her potential was unlimited. When I heard they were casting *The Wiz*, I immediately envisioned Faye as Dorothy. She had that kind of vocal/dramatic charisma. As excited as I was about Faye's talent, though, it was Faye's heart that drew me to her.

"We were all crazy about Faye," remembered Carol Tillery Banks, then married to Ron O'Neal. "Bob always liked smart, independent, and younger women. He thrives on the stimulation of exceptional ladies, and Faye was certainly exceptional. But Bob is a Sagittarius and secretive in his own way. When it comes to women, he's also controlling—or at least he was in those days. Bob's tendency to mold women clashed with the very character of the women he found so attractive. But because they were younger than him, it usually worked for awhile. When the women grew stronger in their independence, the relationships got rocky. Faye was an example of that."

I was living on West End Avenue and Seventy-seventh Street, a neighborhood of faded elegance. Miles Davis lived across the street.

"When we visited Pops during the summers," Kevin recalled, "we were always on the lookout for Miles. Miles was the man. We'd catch a glimpse of the 'Prince of Darkness' floating in or out of his

apartment at strange hours. He symbolized the coolness of black music. More and more, my brother and I were into that music. The
seventies were our high school years when our musical appetites were
whetted. I was playing piano and Jacques was singing. We were into
everyone from Herbie Hancock to Marvin Gaye. Dad encouraged
our interest. During one of his *Purlie* tours, I went along and en-
rolled in correspondence school. Being with Pops was always my first
priority. Jacques was different; he was more comfortable with Mom.
But for both of us, those summers in New York were magic. Jacques
and I wanted what Dad had—a career in music."

My career took a couple of strange twists. In between tours of
*Purlie,* I found myself in two productions worlds apart. The first
was the follow-up film to the spectacular success *Superfly—Superfly
T.N.T.* The second was Shakespeare's *Othello,* in which I played the
Moor. Both performances were less than triumphant.

Ron O'Neal went through heavy changes after the notoriety of
*Superfly.* Here was a serious actor—perhaps the most serious and
talented actor I knew—who was not being taken seriously. That
wounded him. Commercial success was sweet, but his Virgo sensibility was enraged that the highbrows viewed his character with
such contempt. In response, Ron got busy making *Superfly T.N.T.*
In this film, he got to do just what he wanted. Ron wanted to help
his cronies. He made sure that Roscoe Lee Browne had a significant
supporting role and insisted that Alex Haley's screenplay include a
part for me. I was grateful. This was my first Hollywood film. The
box-office prosperity of *Superfly* meant Ron had a big budget for the
sequel. The story was set in Europe and Africa and, for the most part,
was shot on location. I played an expatriate singer looking to make
it in Rome. I had nothing to do with the main story line, but Ron
didn't care. His attitude was, "Goddamnit, this is my movie and I'll
feature my friends." I had one dramatic scene, in which I got up and
sang "O Sole Mio" in a restaurant. It is not a happy memory. I milked

the occasion for more than it was worth and wound up oversinging, an habitual flaw I still lacked the objectivity to check. Ron himself lacked the objectivity to see that Haley's script was flawed. (There was, however, a single exchange of dialogue between me and Ron that I relish: After getting to know my character, Superfly says, "I didn't know you'd turn out to be black." I respond, "I didn't either.")

This was the era of Pan-Africanism, and I'm afraid Ron imposed a political agenda on a sketchy story. The result was a fractured film that went nowhere. Afterward, Ron struggled. He was never offered another major starring role. The culture was saying, *We got one black movie star, Sidney Poitier, and we sure don't need another.* Ron's meteoric rise to superstardom had both emboldened and confused him. His inability to create a franchise with the character—à la James Bond—made further success impossible. He felt like he had blown it, and, in a sad twist of irony, embraced some of Superfly's self-destructive tendencies. Ron had a hard time handling Hollywood.

On a different track, I wondered whether I could handle Shake-speare. I was asked to play Othello in a lavish outdoor production on the great Mall in the heart of monumental Washington, D.C. I accepted eagerly. I love the play, which I don't view as a black/white confrontation. Here in the U.S., any dark character in an all-Caucasian cast is assumed to be ensnared in a racial dilemma. But I don't believe Shakespeare viewed the Moor primarily as a black man, but rather as an outsider. He was delineating the prejudice with which English society regarded anyone who wasn't English, anyone outside the ethnic mainstream. In that regard, I relate completely. Othello is vulnerable to deep insecurities and inner rages, which he himself fails to understand. He questions his ability to express himself—"Rude I am in my speech," he declaims, "and little blessed with the soft phrase of peace"—even as he realizes it's his storytelling that woos and wins Desdemona. Listening to Othello tell her father the story of his life, Desdemona is enraptured.

Othello's duality—strong and weak, secure and insecure, bold and frightened—appeals to the duality within me. I also love the language. I wish I could say that I studied and mastered iambic pentameter. I did not. I'm not even certain I understood the metric integrity of the lines. But I am sure I felt the sentiment behind them. I moved through the play instinctively, easing into a cadence that seemed both reasonable and real. Just as Othello beguiled Desdemona, so did I attempt to beguile the audience. Whatever delusions of grandeur I might have harbored, however, were shattered by a group of uninvited spectators.

The play was to run for two months in summer, a season when the nation's capital is overrun with tourists. We rehearsed on the outdoor set for several weeks. Our final dress rehearsal took place on a hot Friday afternoon, anticipating our opening that night. I couldn't help but notice a group of young black kids who'd ridden their bikes over to check us out. I was in full costume, and they looked at me as if to say, "Why is this black dude in this white play?" Their scrutiny made me uncomfortable. I hoped they would not return for the performance. Evening came. A large crowd showed up on the lawn of the Mall, bringing blankets and picnic baskets, wine and cheese. It was a sophisticated gathering. Somewhere in Act V, I heard the sound of bike bells and knew the boys had arrived. Their presence rattled me. After killing Desdemona, I should have said, "My wife! My wife! What wife? I have no wife," but instead said, "What wife? I ain't got no wife." Minutes later, when, in impassioned confusion, I asked myself, "O, where should Othello go?" one of the boys yelled out, in a voice louder than mine, "Back to Ethiopia, motherfucker!"

Back to Broadway. In the mid-seventies, in what turned out to be the biggest break of my highly uneven career, I was cast in an all-black revival of *Guys and Dolls*. Damon Runyon, of course, was the great bard of Broadway. One of his short stories, "The Idyll of Miss

Sarah Brown," provided the plot, which revolved around a floating crap game. The show, starring Robert Alda, Vivian Blaine, and Sam Levene, opened in 1950 and ran for twelve hundred performances. Five years later, the movie starred Marlon Brando, Frank Sinatra, Jean Simmons, and Vivian Blaine. Frank Loesser captured the delicatessen flavor of Runyon's fiction in a series of delightful songs. *Guys and Dolls* is among the most beloved of Broadway musicals.

In the revival, I played Nathan Detroit, and my friend and roommate Jimmy Randolph was Sky Masterson. In some sense, Detroit is the center of action; it's a juicy part. The money was even juicier—fifteen hundred dollars a week. Sixteen years after I had arrived in New York practically penniless, I found myself earning a princely sum. I was well aware that top stars—Sammy Davis or Jackie Gleason —might earn five thousand dollars weekly, but that in no way detracted from what I saw as a financial windfall. And yet . . .

I liked singing the songs; I liked the commanding the stage; I liked being nominated for a Tony (although I did not win). What I distinctly did not like, though, was the idea of an all-black cast imposed upon what had been an all-white musical. In America, the idea only seems to come up in conjunction with blacks. I ask myself why. Remnants of minstrelsy hang in the air. One thinks of blackface white entertainers. In this case, the reversal—blacks playing white-faced characters—is supposedly benevolent. The annoying assumption, though, is that we can't play whites; we must reinvent the characters as blacks. It feels like forced segregation. The truth is that there was nothing black about Runyon's story or Loesser's songs. We played it straight—and it worked because, I dare say, we could act. After seeing my performance, actor Ron Liebman told me I'd managed to be black and Jewish at the same time. I accepted the compliment, yet all I was doing was speaking the King's English. Perhaps, through osmosis, my years in the Catskills had affected me in ways I didn't understand. But I doubt it. I was sure as hell a lot less Jewish than Sam Levene, though maybe a little more Jewish than Frank Sinatra.

The point is that the underlying convention—doing Runyon with an all-black cast—was absurd but not necessarily unworkable.

Yet it was precisely this absurdity that fueled the fires of my career. In fact, absurdity became something of an operating principle. Certain theatrical absurdities radically changed my life in ways I could have never anticipated. If I had once worshipped logic, I now knew that such worship was misplaced. Logic would not take me from point A to point B. The wiles of show business and the peculiarities of American pop culture were the real forces at play. Those were forces that, despite my efforts, I could never control. The question, then, was simple: Could I, like the willow, bend with the breeze? Or would I, being a stubborn son-of-a-bitch, snap?

# Stone Love

In the seventies, while I was shifting attention from Othello to Nathan Detroit, my sons, Kevin and Jacques, were becoming young men. Because Jacques is no longer here—and because I was absent for most of his upbringing—I've asked his closest family and friends to help relate his remarkable story.

"I met Jacques our first day of high school," said Jerome Davis. "We sat on the bus together and bonded right away. He said he wanted to sing, and so did I. We talked about starting a group. Jacques was full of positive energy and bright ideas. He was a bass with a spectacularly good voice and a great ear for harmony. High school was all about singing. We started out at an all-boys Catholic school but later transferred to a public school because that's where the girls were. Jacques was a magnet for pretty girls."

"Jacques was extremely handsome," remembered his first cousin Carla Caldwell. "He was blessed with a beautiful bubbly personality and fantastic humor. Jacques would crack you up. He had this funny way of walking on his toes. He had his own style. In high school, everyone wanted to be with Jacques. The five-man group he formed with Jerome was called Stone Love, and those boys could flat-out sing. In the little world of St. Louis high schools, they were stars. They wore hip blue derbies and studded jean outfits with 'Stone Love' and peace signs emblazoned in rhinestones across the back."

"Jacques was our leader," said Jerome. "His charisma got us over. We had a flashy show—strong singing, fancy steppin', the whole package. We'd cover the big hits by the O'Jays and Dramatics and

Spinners. Jacques's idol was Jeffrey Osborne of LTD. Seems like Jacques sang 'Love Ballad' better than Jeffrey. We loved the gospel-soul style so much that we joined Union Tabernacle, a Baptist church, just because the music was so hot. We tore up 'Lean On Me' in the choir."

"Jacques was smart as a whip," recalled Carla. "He stayed on the honor roll. He had one of those sunshine personalities that lit up your day. He'd wake up singing. He kept me happy. His mom and my mom are sisters, and Jacques was as close to me as a brother."

"You had to admire my brother," said Kevin. "He was a performer. Stone Love was the bomb. About the same time, I had a fusion band called Cosmo, based on Weather Report. Our stuff tended to be intellectual; Stone Love was out-and-out emotional. They were somewhere between the Temptations and Blue Magic. Each of the guys could sing lead. They could squawl, they could sing falsetto, and, with the right manager, they could have had a hit. That manager never came along, and, sometime after graduation, Stone Love fizzled out.

"This is the same time zone when my brother was questioning his sexuality. St. Louis is—or at least was—provincial when it comes to alternative lifestyles. Early on, Jacques's sensitivity was evident. He was different. His sexual preference, though, remained ambiguous for a long time."

"You have to remember that Stone Love was a group of superfine brothers with big beautiful Afros," Carla commented. "They drove the girls crazy. They even had groupies. Jacques had many girlfriends. He took a beautiful girl to the prom. His family might have had suspicions about his sexuality, but we never voiced them. It was none of our business. Jacques was a plainspoken and completely candid person. He didn't pull punches. When it was time for him to say something, he'd say it. But this was a part of his life that he kept private. Emotionally, we didn't know what he was going through."

"The seventies were years of sexual experimentation," said Jerome. "After high school, the experimentation widened. I went to the

University of Missouri in Columbia, and Jacques went to Fontbonne, a Catholic college in St. Louis. He got a job at the government record center and wasn't really sure of what to do with his life. He was a natural-born singer, and St. Louis seemed too small to contain his ambitions. But unlike Kevin, Jacques was never close to his dad. He didn't know how to reach out for help, and I'm not sure his dad knew what was going on."

I didn't. I was fixated on my own career. I knew my sons possessed musical talent but wasn't sure how—or whether it was my place—to push them. I figured that, like me, they'd find their own way. Unfortunately, my approach with Faye was less laissez-faire. I did push her to seek roles that I felt suited her great talent. Over the long course of our relationship, she won several plum parts, but I always felt she should do more. I imposed my ambition upon her own more balanced sense of life. She responded with bemusement; she knew I was driven by forces that were peculiar to me. She put up with me. I realized that she was a superior person, but I'm not sure I understood the depth of her emotional commitment to our relationship. The fact that I still hadn't divorced Marlene after twenty years says much about my inability to commit. My one and only marriage protected me from any other. It kept me from facing an unpleasant truth about myself: Even when I enjoyed the sexual, romantic, and intellectual favors of women of the caliber of Karin Berg and Faye Hauser, I couldn't respond with my heart. My heart remained hidden. My head, if not my genitals, led the way. The way, however, was not entirely clear.

In the seventies, that great American television form, the half hour sitcom, went through a critical change. Revolutionary attitudes set in motion in the sixties were manifesting themselves in mainstream pop culture. A prime example was *All in the Family,* Norman Lear's send-up of a white working man caught in the crossfire of social change. Lear was a liberal who allowed the arch conservative Archie Bunker his full measure of humanity. Bunker was a bigot, but a funny bigot.

Humor was mined from the very ridiculousness of his prejudice. I thought it was an ingenious way to point out the folly of intolerance. It was also an across-the-board hit. After *Julia*, I'd made a guest appearance on *Marcus Welby, M.D.*, playing a political militant, but getting a part on *All in the Family*, then ranked number one, was even more of a score.

The situation was typical: Archie has a medical emergency, rushes to a street clinic, and demands to see the first available doctor. That's my character. Of course he's horrified at the idea of being treated— and touched—by a black man. As I examine him, he mumbles racist remarks. He expresses an unfamiliarity with the texture of black hair, setting up my big line: "You can rub my head if you want to." I delivered it with a kind of studied simplicity. The study involved the art of minimalism. Wait a couple of beats, then say little. The audience howled. It was another instance in which I viewed television acting as a Zen exercise in restraint. On stage, you go to the audience; on TV, you let the camera (which is, of course, the audience) come to you. I further saw how blacks may have a peculiar affinity for the medium. In the long and complex history of black/white relations, verbal restraint became a necessary tool. Speaking our displeasure could get us killed. Similarly, the black comic was restricted in what he could say to his white colleague, who was invariably his employer. Facial expression was utilized where verbal expression was prohibited. Blacks became adept at what I call mumbling on the face. Widening our eyes, raising our eyebrows, turning down our mouths, turning up our smiles—all techniques that enlarged our acting arsenal. How else could we express irony or disapproval, sarcasm or dissent? When it came time to do TV, where tight camera shots focused on subtle facial expressions that would have been invisible to theater audiences, we had already developed nonverbal expertise—and instinctively knew how to employ it.

The idea of high-paying television employment was tempting, especially as more blacks were introduced on more programs. Flip

Wilson and Bill Cosby were all over TV; Redd Foxx had his own show; *Good Times, What's Happening!* and *The Jeffersons* were hits. Could I reinvent myself as a funnyman? Certainly not. I never thought I was very funny. I was too stiff, square, and self-conscious. Yet *All in the Family* proved that, taking my time and playing it straight, I could make an audience laugh. Within a comic framework, I had a good sense of when to speak, when to stay silent. Television was fine, but I didn't see it as my future.

# Dinner for Four

Faye and I were dining with Ron O'Neal and his wife, Carol Tillery Banks, at the Villa Taxco restaurant in Los Angeles. I'd come to Hollywood to audition for a new TV sitcom, our topic of conversation that night as we passed around the tacos. I was uneasy about the situation. Back in New York, after a successful run, *Guys and Dolls* was closing. I needed work, and when my agent at William Morris called me about a new ABC show called *Soap*, I was interested. The agent, though, was skeptical. "There's a part for a butler/cook, but I'm afraid you're too old. Besides, they're favoring a Japanese woman." I also had reservations about the role. After all, my grandmother had been a servant whose dream was to see me as anything *but* a servant. No, it would not be my first choice for a role on national TV. On the other hand, when I read the script, I saw *Soap* as a cutting-edge comedy, a biting satire on the American WASP. It turned the American family on its head and reveled in irony. "I can get you an audition," my agent promised, "but I wouldn't get my hopes up." As I saw it, if I got the role, I could always turn it down. I decided to fly out to L. A. and go for it. Tomorrow was the audition; tonight was dinner at Villa Taxco.

It had been four years since Ron's *Superfly* exploded on screens around the world. *Superfly T.N.T.*, with my infamous "O Sole Mio," had bombed. Since then, Ron's career had cooled considerably, though his radicalism was still fiery hot.

"It's insulting," he insisted. "You're beyond playing a cook. I'm telling you, Bob, it's a step backwards. Television is still operating in the dark ages of Amos and Andy."

Carol vehemently disagreed. "We all know how tricky this business can be. We have to grab what we can. Besides, it's not so much the part itself, but what Bob can do with it."

"Bullshit," Ron retorted. "Demeaning is demeaning. You can't change that."

Faye sided with Carol. "I'm from the South," she said, "and I know dozens of domestics who do their work with dignity. If it's not beneath them to work as domestics, why should it be beneath us to play domestics? My NAACP background says you keep on plugging. You do what you can; you take what roles come your way; you make the best of a system that offers you few chances. Why blow a good chance?"

"Because," Ron answered, "anything's better than perpetuating a rotten system."

"And who's going to pay Bob's rent," Carol asked Ron. "You?"

I took it all in and said little. "It's all academic," I reflected, "if I don't get the goddamn part."

I showed up the next morning with something of a mantra in mind: "Do Nothing." It was advice I had started to give actors who came to me lamenting their inability to score. At age fifty, I'd finally figured out something about my own auditions—I tried too hard. Most actors do. It's understandable. Our desperation is never far from the surface. We desperately want to win the role; we need the work; we need to succeed. The desperation is fueled by fear. There are hundreds, thousands more actors than roles. In the face of such daunting odds, how can we help but feel—and act—needy? Once in the room, once facing the director making the decision, we do everything to please but stand on our heads. We frantically try to figure out what the director wants and, in doing so, stray from our dramatic instincts. We leave the core of ourselves to wander into uncharted territory. In seeking acceptance, we abandon our souls. We lose focus. Directors smell our desperation and dismiss us out of hand.

So what's the alternative? "Do Nothing." Show up. Give up specu-
lating about what *they* want. Concentrate on what *you* feel. Concentrate on simply being there. Being present. Being in the process of
reading lines as best you can. Jazz drummers know, for example, that
anticipating the beat kills any chance of swing. You let the beat come
to you. Auditions are much the same. If you jump on the beat, if you
jump on the lines, if, in short, you try too hard, you're likely to fall on
your ass.

"Do Nothing" was much on my mind as I approached the reading. I
had heard that, although the part was written for a black man, other
auditioners had been either too militant or too obsequious. That's
why they were considering a Japanese woman instead. I understood
the dilemma. For a black man, the material was complex. The character was irreverent. The question was, how to express such irreverence?
In reading the lines, I felt an immediate rapport with this butler called
Benson. He was doing what he had to do, but he didn't particularly
like it. He expressed the kind of disdain I associated with my brother,
James. Like my grandmother, James was not one to suffer fools, no
matter where he worked. James was aloof. And of course my grandmother, whether mopping a floor or washing a shirt, was the absolute
queen of her domain. She feared no employer. These were attitudes
deeply imbedded in me; they were the absolute core of my childhood,
my initial and indelible exposure to the tension between white employer and black employee. Benson was my brother; Benson was my
grandmother; Benson, with only a few twists of fate, was me.

My mind was flooded with memories. As a child, I had seen the
work of the black comics of the day—Mantan Moreland, Willie Best,
Step 'n Fetchit. On television, I had watched Rochester wash Jack
Benny's car. I understood that these guys did what they did because
they had to. I understood it was political. I also understood no fool
could play a fool; it required cunning and intelligence. I respected
these actors' talent and empathized with their dramatic dilemma. At

the same time, seeing them in the films of the forties, I had felt a tinge of shame; I wondered why these were the only images being projected. I knew that blacks who did menial tasks did not see themselves as undignified. I knew that because I myself had done such tasks. The truth was that blacks invariably brought to such work skill and the saving grace of ironic humor. I was also committed to speaking the language well. Any deviation from eloquent English had to be well founded on solid dramatic ground. I had no interest in playing characters like those I had seen as a child—self-mocking, self-pitying, or self-demeaning. I wanted the job, yes, but I was hell-bent on making a positive contribution. I wanted black people to be proud of Benson.

*Soap*'s sarcastic take on society served my purpose and suited my sensibility. My rage, like Benson's, stayed on the surface and was easily provoked. If I even suspected someone considered me stupid, my back arched and my tongue attacked. As I read the part during the audition, I elicited laughs by following my mantra—*Do Nothing*. I was aloof, allowing my verbal darts to land where they might. One of the directors was concerned that my attitude was too caustic and suggested that I soften my stingers with an implied, "Just kidding." When I employed that device, though, the laughs stopped. Everyone saw that my initial instinct—to simply let the character be, without qualification or apology—worked like a charm. I was called back for a second reading. By then, I felt like I had the character in my hip pocket. I knew this man. A week or so passed. I returned to New York. Then the call came. I got the job.

Benson changed my life. The salary—some thirty-five hundred dollars an episode—was enough to allow me to move from New York to Los Angeles, thus spinning my career in a new direction. While I was certainly not rich, I was making more money than ever before—and being viewed by millions more people than had ever seen me on stage. All these were pluses. And the show itself, while not Ibsen or Shakespeare, was extremely funny, even groundbreaking. Not to mention a solid hit.

The ensemble was superb. Katherine Helmond, Robert Mandan, Diana Canova, Richard Mulligan, Jennifer Salt, Jimmy Baio, Arthur Peterson, and Billy Crystal (playing the first gay in sitcom history) formed a wildly confused version of a supposedly upstanding American family in Dunn's River, Connecticut. The only unconfused character is Benson. He socks it to everyone. He was based on a butler who had worked for Danny Thomas and helped raise the Thomas children, one of whom—Tony Thomas—was an executive producer of the team, Witt-Thomas-Harris, that created the show. Susan Harris was the writer, a savvy woman with a deep understanding of what makes sitcoms funny. She forged my character against type. She knew she wanted him surly; beyond that, he was still unformed when I stepped into the role. I hope it doesn't sound self-serving to say that I gave Benson the attitude that made him who he was. He was simply one of those characters—Archie Bunker, George Jefferson, and Maude were others—whom actors enlarge and ultimately inhabit.

Benson also became a fictional mirror of my own psyche. I had pursued acting, after all, because I saw it as a profession where I was not beholden to anyone. Benson saw his job the same way. In the first episode, when his female employer comes into the kitchen to ask what he's doing, he doesn't mince words. "What does it look like I'm doing? Making eggs." The fact that he knows that eggs are injurious to his male employer's health, yet continues scrambling them, underlines Benson's role as a subversive. His subversiveness made the part a pleasure. That, and the good money, annihilated any arguments about whether I should or should not play a servant. More and more, I saw Benson as Mantan Moreland's revenge.

If there was any danger, it was in the intensity of that revenge. Or was it revenge? I'm not sure I was motivated by reprisal. I am sure, though, that my old attitudes had not abated. If I thought a director's comments were intelligent, I would respond positively. If I did not respect the direction, I wouldn't respond at all. Or I would argue. Little Robert Williams, who had fought the priests at St. Nick's, was still inside me—the same Robert Williams who had ferociously debated professors at Washington University or mocked impresario Marcel Prawy in Vienna. That obstinate fool was still capable of undermining any authority he confronted. Now, though, faced with the chance of a major success, I took stringent measures to check the fool. I did it in crude fashion. I knew the fool would not respond to anything less than a full frontal assault.

A director, for example, might make a suggestion that I found less than astute. Rather than ignore it, I was tempted to castigate the man, to tongue-lash and ridicule him before the entire cast and crew. For someone whose career had taken a positive new turn, this was self-destructive. The director might be important in the TV community; he might have connections to dozens of producers. He could get me more work, or he could put out the word that I was an impossible bastard. The choice was mine. When such moments occurred, I excused myself from the set and marched into the men's room. There I made sure I was alone. I stood before the mirror. I counted to ten. I looked at my reflection long and hard. And then I said, *"Shut the fuck up, Guillaume. Just shut the fuck up."*

*"Shut the fuck up,"* like *"Do Nothing,"* became a constant mantra. Protecting myself from myself became an ongoing chore. I was blessed that my opportunity for TV success came after I'd reached middle age. God knows I needed all those years to gain some objectivity. Self-defeating mechanisms are subtle and pernicious. You shoot yourself in the foot, and you're not even sure where you got the gun. My friend Ron O'Neal, for instance, an actor as talented as any I have known, struggled with that very mystery. At the end of the seventies, he made a movie with Kirk Douglas called *The Final Countdown,* but I think he slowly lost his footing in Hollywood. To stay on solid ground is no easy trick for a black actor—for any actor. After a lifetime of uncertainty, I wanted solidity. To attain it, I fought myself. I stared

myself down. I became my own authority, my own teacher, my own father, my own disciplinarian. I wouldn't take any shit. *"Shut the fuck up, Guillaume. Just shut the fuck up."*

In 1979, in my second year on *Soap*, I won an Emmy as outstanding supporting actor in a comedy. In 1980, ABC made the decision to give Benson a show of his own. "This," the producers promised me, "will make you a bona fide star."

# Pat Carpenter

"The first time I saw my father he was on TV with Diahann Carroll in *Julia*. That was the late sixties when I was eighteen and already married. My husband, Odie, remembers that I pronounced my father's name *Goulet*. 'Robert Goulet can't be your father,' he said, 'he's white.' It took me awhile to learn the correct pronunciation of Guillaume. I could never convince my friends that the man on TV was really my dad. On one hand, it was exciting to know I had a famous father, but demoralizing and frustrating when no one believed that I was his daughter. The truth is that the man was no more real to me than a ghost. He had never called me, never said a word to me, never tried to contact me. Not once.

"My mother was Mary, the woman with whom my father had a brief affair in 1949. I was born in 1950. My mother's sister Matty was married to my father's brother, James. Their son, Jerry, was two years older than me. Just before I was six, my mother was killed in a car accident. Jerry's mother, Matty, suffered with mental illness and was frequently hospitalized. She and James divorced when Jerry and I were kids. Jerry and I had a unique relationship: Our mothers were sisters and our fathers were brothers, yet all four parents had either died, disappeared or visited only infrequently. It was our mothers' parents, Grandma and Grandpa, who raised us.

"My grandfather had a strong dislike for my father. He didn't really know him, but he didn't have to. To my grandfather, my father was simply the man who had impregnated his daughter and jumped ship. Whenever my father was mentioned, it was with resentment and anger. The connection to my father's family, though, was never entirely broken. Uncle James's second wife, Leona, was close to my grandmother. Through Leona and James, I met my aunt Cleo. She was a troubled lady, but her heart was good as gold. I got to know Cleo's children, my cousins Rikki and Kandyce. I saw Cleo as another link to my father. She made it seem as though she and her glamorous brother were close. In 1971, when I saw in the paper that Robert Guillaume was appearing in St. Louis as the star of *Purlie*, I asked Cleo if she could take me to the show and introduce me to my father, whom I still had yet to meet. 'Of course,' she said. 'He'd like that.'

"I was thrilled. I counted the days before the show opened. Imagined what meeting him would be like. Waited for the phone to ring. But it never did. Cleo never called. I never got to see my father, much less meet him. Turned out Cleo was not as close to him as she had led me to believe. The experience left me devastated. Even more devastating was the drive-by murder of Jerry in 1976. When his father, James, who had then moved to Los Angeles, came to St. Louis for the funeral, the subject of his brother, Robert, came up again. 'I've been working at the L. A. airport where I ran into Bob,' James told me. 'I talked about you. Told him you were a fine young woman. Told him he'd be proud. Said he needed to see you.' My heart began racing. 'And what did he say?' I asked. 'He just smiled.'

"In 1977, with *Soap* on TV every week, my father was always on my mind. I could no longer ignore or forget him. Everyone was talking about the show. Then one evening I got a call from Leona and James, saying that my father was on his way to their house in L. A. They wanted me to wait an hour and then call. I was excited, confused, nervous, hopeful, skeptical, afraid—every emotion you can name. An hour passed. I picked up the phone and dialed. Waited for the first ring, then the second, then the third. On the fourth ring, James picked up. 'Is that you, Pat?' he asked. 'It's me.' 'Okay, sugar, let me give the phone to your father.' My voice was shaking; his was deep and strong. Can't remember a word we said. The conversation was brief. He was nice but a little matter-of-fact. Later I learned that, after hanging up, he called his sister Cleo to make sure that I was, in fact, his daughter. She assured him I was. A week passed. I didn't know what to think. Would another twenty-seven years go by without hearing from him again? Would I *ever* hear from him again? Then he called. 'I'd like to have you and your family out to L. A.,' he said. 'I'm sending you tickets.' I was overjoyed.

"Came time for the trip. Odie, myself, and our two kids—Ava was six, Anthony was ten—got on the plane and flew to California. All the time I'm wondering what it's going to be like to meet this man, this ghost who appears on TV but not in real life. Now this is real life. Now the plane's landing. 'Look, Pat,' says Odie. 'If we get off as a family, he'll know it's us. So why don't you get off first—alone—and see if he recognizes you.' I did. Went down the walkway with my heart racing like crazy. Soon as I saw him, our visions locked. He knew me. Came up and embraced me. A lifetime of waiting, a lifetime of wondering, a lifetime of wanting a father. I wept on his shoulder, and he held me; he welcomed me into his life.

"He was living with Faye Hauser in a house in Laurel Canyon they were renting from Ron O'Neal. Faye was a beautiful person and wonderful actress. She played the schoolteacher in *Roots: The Next Generation.* Her life with my father seemed terribly glamorous to me. I felt like an outsider, but he did his best to make me feel welcome. Little by little I started calling him Dad. I could see that he was a good person looking to do the right thing. From then on, he had us out two or three times a year. That initial year, though, wasn't easy. After the initial joy of being acknowledged as his daughter, I had hard resentments to work through. Why had he left me? Where had he been? Why had he never asked about me or looked for me? How could he be so cold? Didn't I count for anything?

"To Dad's credit, he sat and listened to my emotional explosions. He let me go off. Let me ventilate. Didn't try to argue or justify. He knew I needed to be heard—by him. He gave me the time and space and never flinched when my accusations flew right at him. He apologized. Said he was glad I was in his life. Said from now, we'd be family. He embraced my husband as a son. At first, he hated being called 'Grandpa'—that made him feel old—but he eventually warmed to the notion and was great with my kids. Ironically, Dad turned out to be someone with great love for children.

"For people who were estranged their entire lives, we were remarkably harmonious. There was natural rapport between us. He respected the fact that I was a public aid caseworker, and I respected his skill as a professional actor. He had a dignity about him that everyone admired. The only thing I didn't admire, though, was the fact that his life was compartmentalized. It infuriated me, for instance, that he still hadn't told his sons, Kevin and Jacques, that they had a sister. He thought he could go on seeing me and my family without letting his other children know I had entered his life. Part of me understood. Revealing my existence meant admitting a secret he had buried for twenty-seven years. Formally, he was still married to Marlene. Not even she knew the truth. But the truth is the truth, I argued. It was preposterous to expect me to go back to St. Louis, where my brothers lived, and not want to meet them. If I was part of Dad's life, I wanted to be part of theirs as well. A wise soul once said, 'We're only as sick as our secrets.' Well, I no longer wanted to be a secret. I no longer wanted the shame. It was time for everyone to know the truth. It took a few months, but Dad did it. He called Jacques and Kevin and said they had a sister. Not long after, I went to meet them. It was a lot less nerve-racking than meeting Dad. It was as though we'd known each other forever. The connection was immediate. They were wonderful guys, bright and creative and amazingly accepting. We clicked. We felt the joy of family and remained close from that first day on."

I cannot claim credit for putting together my fractured family. That was entirely Pat's doing. Left to my own devices, I would have surely left things as they were. Conjuring up the past has never been easy for me, especially regarding family. The fact that I had a daughter crossed my mind over the years, but I quickly dismissed the thought. I preferred to be left alone; I wasn't looking for complications, emotional or otherwise. On the other hand, when James and Leona urged me to speak to Pat, I could hardly refuse. It was painful to be reminded of my extreme negligence; surely that's why I had avoided the matter. I had stuffed my guilt into the recesses of my mind. But when Pat got off the plane, when I saw this bright and engaging young woman, when I got to know her husband and kids, I quickly realized I had not only been denying her, I had been denying myself. She and her family enriched my life. She also had psychological insights I lacked. Pat understood that it would help us all if Kevin and Jacques knew about her. I had to fight my fear of looking like a rat; I didn't want to tell my sons about their sister. That little baby girl I had abandoned was now facing me in the form of an accomplished twenty-seven-year-old woman. This was a woman who knew far more about the healing nature of family than I. It was not pleasant to hear her resentments. No one enjoys being taken to task, especially when accusations are true and anger justified. I sat there and listened to my daughter because I realized she was right. Her passion to create a family that included me was greater than my inclination to escape. I had been escaping emotional involvement my entire life. In many ways, I would continue to escape. But in this vital area of parenthood, I was made to stop and reexamine myself. After a few months, the truth became clear: the arrival of my daughter, and the moral imperative she embodied, was a blessing.

As a rule, I have not been blessed with great psychological insight. I have ruined any number of good relationships. The most dramatic ruination involved Faye Hauser. It all happened at what should have been the happiest moment in my life. I was a celebrity. I was becoming wealthy. For more than twenty years, I had fought the brutal show biz wars. Finally I had won. Or had I?

# Brother, Sister, Mother

While Faye and I faced our crisis as a couple, other crises faced my family. They involved my brother, James, and my sister Cleo. James had it rough. His dishonorable discharge from the navy was a trauma he never overcame. Acting was an outlet for much of my rage. James had no such outlet. He was a marvelous trumpeter and pianist, but he never pursued those talents. I had defended him before his teachers when we were kids, but as an adult I was never much comfort to him. Yet when he moved to Los Angeles, we reconnected. I was grateful that he and his wife, Leona, set up my meeting with Pat. And I found myself eager to rekindle the warmth that had once flowed between us. James never realized his dreams, but he was coping. He supervised a crew of workers who parked cars at LAX, and his bitterness had subsided. I'd go over to his house—and he'd come to mine—and it was almost like old times. We laughed at each other's jokes, we put up with each other's foibles, we enjoyed the exclusive camaraderie of brothers. James knew me like no one else. Because so much of his personality was at play in my rendition of Benson, it was a particular pleasure to be in his company. Unfortunately, the good times didn't last. The death of his son, Jerry, was a terrible blow. Not long after, James suffered a debilitating stroke. He was still in his early fifties; he'd live another ten years, but virtually without speech or mobility. We had found each other, only to lose each other.

My sister Cleo had long been losing her health to drugs. This lovely and intelligent woman had, like my mother, fallen victim to the mysterious sickness of substance abuse. Because I was so adamant about keeping my distance from my family—and especially from my mother—I missed the final chapter in Bunk and Cleo's complex relationship. I regret that. I especially regret how my fear of inserting myself into familial matters kept me from an extraordinary transformation: Bunk changed utterly; her reformation was dramatic and heartfelt. But it is not for me to tell the story, since I was too far away—emotionally and geographically—to witness the phenomenon. It was my mother's grandchildren—Cleo's sons Rikki, Ronald, and Kenneth, and her daughter, Kandyce—who felt the repercussions most closely.

"My mother's drug addiction became clear to us when we were very young," said Rikki. "She'd tell us, 'I'll be right back,' and then be gone for weeks. When my mother fell short, though, her mother picked up the slack. They called my grandmother Bunk, but we called her Big Mama. She truly became our mother."

"I heard stories about Big Mama when she was young," Kandyce remembered. "They said she had her wild ways, and I know Uncle Robert had little to do with her after he left St. Louis. They say she was cruel and irresponsible, but, believe me, I never knew that person. Big Mama was loving and nurturing, everything a little kid could want or need."

"Big Mama and Cleo had their squabbles," said Rikki. "My grandmother desperately wanted her daughter to avoid the mistakes she herself had made. But it wasn't to be. When Big Mama saw she couldn't change Cleo, she replaced her in our household. In 1969, when my mother went to rehab, Big Mama moved in and stayed. In 1973, Cleo contracted emphysema. She was only forty-four. She lived another thirteen years. She held good jobs for awhile and helped others who had problems, but her own struggles continued. It was Big Mama who held our family together, working as a waitress, making sure we were provided for. When the chips were down, Big Mama came through."

"For most of my childhood," said Kandyce, "I'd watch my mother go out on binges. I watched her destroy herself. As she grew weaker,

Big Mama grew stronger. We all owe her our lives and sanity. I have no doubt that my mother was a good woman. But that goodness was overpowered by a lifetime of self-abuse. She struggled to care for her own children. Big Mama provided that care. Big Mama saved us."

When Bunk died of a heart attack in 1980 at age seventy-two, I still didn't know her. I didn't know of her reformation. My childhood scars had not sufficiently healed. I might have been foolish; I might have been unforgiving; I tried to assuage my guilt by sending her money the last ten years of her life; I tried to comfort myself with the thought that, while I couldn't afford to bury my grandmother, I could and did give Bunk a respectable burial. I attended. I may have wept on the inside, but my eyes were dry. Even at her death, I felt the gap between us. I yearned to love her, to understand and forgive her, to realize that she, like all of us, had done the best she could. I suppose that by attending I did the best I could. To do more was beyond me.

I isolated myself in California much the way I had isolated myself in New York. My focus was on work. Situation comedies are demanding; the work is arduous, the hours long, the preparation exacting. I thrived in such a climate. Now that I had achieved success and a degree of artistic control, my dedication to the task was absolute. Benson was my man. I saw to it that he rose in position and status. When he left *Soap*, he went to work for the governor on *Benson*. Over the seven years he was on the air, he went from being a butler to a budget director to lieutenant governor. The implication was that he would soon be governor himself. Without sacrificing his salty humor, I fought for his dignity. I even fought for his wardrobe. When he stepped out of the governor's mansion, the producers wanted him to wear a certain nondescript suit. I refused to go along. "Saville Row is not his style," they said. "Neither is Catfish Row," I countered. They did not think that was funny, but they relented. It was a heady time. Over the next six years, I would receive five Emmy nominations as outstanding lead actor in a comedy series and win the honor once, in 1985. My savvy manager, Phil Margo, had cut a deal that earned me one hundred thousand dollars an episode plus a hefty slice of the show's profits. It was hard to conceive of so much money. At one point, I considered asking my accountants to convert a year's income to cash, stuff it in a big shopping bag, and dump all the bills on my bed. Part of me wanted to see it—to feel it.

Fame is a subtle drug. You may not think you're high; you may believe—as I believed—that your conservative self is taking it all in stride. Yet when the world treats you differently, when the world rewards you extravagantly, when you find yourself buying a suburban home big enough to house half the neighborhood you grew up in, you change. Your attitude is altered. The notion of entitlement takes on new meaning. This was especially true when it came to women. Never before had I had such access to female favors. As a celebrity, it seemed as though I could have any woman I wished for. I wished for many. In following my unchecked passion, I betrayed Faye. It was a time in my life when I was flying high. I paid no attention to the moves I made until after I had made them. And wound up with a mess.

"I never thought I'd wind up in Hollywood," said Faye. "I thought there was a far better chance that I'd be a political street performer than TV actress. My personality isn't Hollywood and, for that matter, neither is Bob's. We were a strange couple out there. Given that climate, I'm not sure I was the best companion for him. I wasn't interested in going to parties or giving parties or partying with the right people. I would never be a good show business wife. The idea of being Bob's wife was not important to me. Middle-class conventions seemed foolish to me. I just wasn't made that way. It was enough to be with Bob. I felt we were deeply in love. I was proud of what he had done with Benson; he made more of that character than anyone could have imagined. It was an instance of highly creative acting—and no one but Bob could have pulled that off. I thought our relationship was solid. It was important that I retained my independence. I always contributed money to our household. I appeared on *Good Times* and *What's Happening!* and in *Roots: The Next Generation* I had a scene with Henry Fonda. Bob tried to motivate me to be more aggressive in pursuing more important parts, but not everyone has his drive. Because Hollywood was never my style, I never took full advantage of Bob's status in the community. I went my own way. I made progress, but nothing like Bob. Bob was entering his glory years. Meanwhile, he thought I was squandering my talent. He envisioned me as a superstar. My reluctance to pursue high-profile success created distance between us. I couldn't throw myself in that world the way he could. I was content to live a quieter life."

The quietude did not last. Several years before, while doing *Purlie* in Philadelphia, I had met a stunning woman named Patricia. She came back to my dressing room to generously praise my performance. I was smitten. The attraction between us was palpable. I saw her as a woman worthy of closer examination. There was unfinished business between us. She came to Los Angeles—all this, of course, without Faye's knowledge—where that business was consummated. The physical union was powerful. In 1979, Patricia informed me that she was pregnant. There was no way to hide the news from Faye.

"I'm not the jealous type," said Faye. "My radar had not gone up. I didn't suspect a thing. I believe men can have close nonsexual friendships with women, and I was certain Bob had many such relationships. But the news that he was having a baby with someone else absolutely blindsided me. I was devastated. I'd gone through a similar trauma in high school when my boyfriend told me he'd gotten another girl pregnant. That was bad, but this was worse. I was an adult. Bob and I had been together for years. We lived under the same roof, slept in the same bed, shared a life. As hurtful as the betrayal was, I did not want to end the relationship. I was willing to stay and try to work it out. That's how much I cared for this man. But Bob saw it differently. He felt an obligation to be with the mother of his child. I cried for weeks. The pain of our separation was excruciating."

I look back at this period and see that I was still emotionally co-matose. I did not sufficiently recognize or value Faye's love. My own ability to love remained stymied. My bias against psychotherapy prevented my seeking professional help. I was left to my own devices, which were dubious at best. My confused sense of responsibility told me to try to forge a family with Patricia. For awhile, I provided for Faye. And I bought a large house in Tarzana and asked Patricia to move in. I thought a lovely new domicile would help solidify my new family. Our beautiful daughter, Melissa, was born in 1980. I fell in love with this child but realized my relationship with her mother was not what I wanted. A few months later, I asked Faye to take me back, but it was too late. The damage had been done. I could be neither persuasive nor persistent. The decent thing was to leave her alone. I'd been a dog. Now I was paying the price.

"At that point," Faye remembered, "it was impossible to repair the relationship. The love remained, but the trust was gone. I didn't blame Bob entirely. Obviously he needed something I wasn't providing. Some men need worshipful women. Well, I never worshipped Bob. I was never doting. And after our thing ended, I was never bitter. I went on. I played on *The Young and the Restless* for years. I directed and produced for syndicated TV. I put my life back together."

Meanwhile, Patricia and I fought continually. I was no fun to live with. My career was thriving while my relationship was in shambles. After a few months, Patricia took Melissa and moved out. I was there for them financially; I still am; my daughter remains an important part of my life. But the family I had envisioned evaporated into thin air. When it came to love, I still didn't have a clue.

I hid inside my work, an easy thing to do since my work was all-consuming. I escaped into superficial affairs, a lifelong pattern exacerbated by TV stardom. I may have fancied myself a man of some intellectual depth, but my intellect failed miserably in matters of the heart. Sexual satisfaction coupled with romantic intrigue remained the driving force. Seeking such satisfaction above all else blinded me to the truth about lasting relationships. Endurance depends upon love. And love depends upon giving. The old handbook about women—the one I'd been using since the fifties—was all about how to get, not how to give. That lesson was still off in my distant future. Besides, with my career prospering, why question the old handbook? Why not just forget my doubts in the arms of the next available woman?

# Intellectual Armor

"Maybe because our relationship has always been platonic," said Carol Tillery Banks, "I've stayed close to Bob through the years. In 1980, when Ron O'Neal and I divorced, Bob was a devoted friend. I worked in his production company and helped run his household after the difficult period with Faye and Patricia. We saw each other through hard times. Bob's armor is intellectual. He uses his mind to protect himself from his feelings. It's a survival strategy that kept him together. It may have caused tension, but it worked for him. While other guys who became stars blew their good fortune on drugs and living a crazy lifestyle, Bob's stayed steady. He never overspent, never went hog-wild. Maybe you could call his relationships with women an unchecked addiction; or maybe you could just say he had a wandering eye. I'm not sure. In many ways, Bob is a traditional macho man. His saving grace, though, is his awareness. Most men don't acknowledge their macho. Bob does. He sees himself from a distance. His intelligence allows him—at least from time to time—to detach from himself, criticize himself, and finally look to the light. It took Bob awhile to see what most men never do: that darkness only brings pain."

"I came to California in the early eighties," remembered Karin Berg, "working in the music business. By then I'd achieved a good level of success. Bob was in *Benson* and several times invited me to the set. I took satisfaction in the fact that, after all we'd been through, we were back to being friends. Bob is not a man you can stay angry at. He's too charming. Under his veneer, he's too sweet. After we were no longer lovers, it was easier for us both. We'd talk about books and plays and one another's career. I'd sit in his dressing room while he changed clothes to go on camera. The makeup men looked quizzically as he got undressed in front of me. 'Don't fret,' Bob said, 'this lady has seen me naked before.' In New York, he took me to see *Dreamgirls* and was mobbed during intermission. His celebrity was at its height. I stood back and watched, amused and amazed—after all, this was the guy I'd met a hundred years before in St. Louis, the guy who'd worked as a streetcar driver and come to New York on a hope and a prayer. I thought Bob handled fame graciously. His manners were always impeccable. Underneath, though, I sensed that all was not well. And in typical Bob fashion, he prevented me—and probably everyone else—from seeing what was really wrong."

I'm not sure I knew what was wrong. I'm not sure I fully processed the disastrous conclusion to my long-term relationship with Faye or my short-term arrangement with Melissa's mother. Work was an effective distraction. For me, the eighties were all about work. Ages fifty-three to sixty-three would prove to be the most productive of my life. I didn't have a moment to waste. My instincts said, *Strike while the iron is hot.* I had a name. I had access to other projects. I had an aggressive manager. I had no intention of squandering any opportunity. In addition to *Benson*, I starred in a series of TV movies with Gary Coleman—*The Kid from Left Field, The Kid with a Broken Halo, The Kid with a 200 IQ*—light fare with a heavy payday. In heavier fare, I played Martin Luther King, Jr., in the docudrama *Prince Jack* and Frederick Douglass in the miniseries *North and South.*

My attitude about acting had decidedly improved. As a younger man, I was convinced I had to be the best actor—and singer—in the history of civilization. My artistic ambition was off the chart. By the time I became Benson, I had chilled considerably. I had let go. I was able to adopt a more reasonable and realistic approach. *I am who I am*, I decided. *And that's just fine. I'm competent. I'm confident enough to accept my limitations. I may not be great, but I'm sufficient. Greatness is no longer a concern. Let me just do the job at hand.* The simplicity of such an attitude allowed me to relax in front of the camera. It was a continuation of my "Do Nothing" philosophy. Let the camera come to me. The same applied to scripts. Let the lines come to me. Don't jump on the jokes; don't look for the laughs. Just be. That measure of relaxation made all the difference in the world. I felt it. The audience felt it. My desperation disappeared.

My domestic life changed dramatically at the start of the eighties. In addition to the upheaval with Faye and Patricia, my sons moved to California and into my home. The shift represented a critical change in their lives and mine. I wanted them to live with me, and fortunately they felt the same.

"It was difficult for me when my sons left St. Louis," said Marlene. "But I knew I couldn't—and shouldn't—keep them at home any longer. Their father had become famous. California looked like the promised land to them. They both wanted a career in music, and Hollywood was the best place to pursue it. Besides, it was time their father took over. I'd been their chief caretaker since they were infants. I could use a rest. And though I knew I'd miss them terribly, I accepted the inevitable—now it was Bob's turn."

"The first time Jacques went to L. A.," his cousin Rikki remembered, "Jerome Davis and I went along. The disco era wasn't quite dead, and the town was jumping. Of course we stayed at Uncle Robert's. His house looked like a palace to us. He got us tickets to *Solid Gold* and *Laverne and Shirley*, and we went out partying every night."

"That trip is when Jacques decided his future was in Los Angeles," said Jerome. "He looked around and saw that he wanted to live the life. L. A. was so much more freeing than St. Louis. You could be who you wanted to be in L. A."

"I moved to L. A. in May of 1980," Kevin recalled. "My brother, Jacques, came that September. One of the reasons Pops bought that huge house in Tarzana—it had four fireplaces and a pool—was to accommodate us. He was going through his changes with Patricia. Our little sister, Melissa, was born during this same time. But through it all, Pops kept his cool. His romantic life—and strife—was strictly his own business. He was discreet. He made sure we were comfortable. Meanwhile, I started working at a music company and Jacques worked as a page at ABC, a job Pops helped him get. But that's about all the help Jacques accepted from my father. As he pursued his singing career over the next seven or eight years, Jacques was reluctant to use Pops's contacts. Jacques was a lot like my father—fiercely independent. He went to Phil Moore, the great vocal teacher who had schooled Lena Horne and Dorothy Dandridge, and began to make serious strides.

"At some point in the early eighties, my brother and I changed our name. Kevin Williams and Jacques Williams became Kevin Guillaume and Jacques Guillaume. I suppose that marked the official changeover in our lives. If we were going to be L. A., if we were going to be in our father's house and work in our father's industry, why not take our father's name? Seemed silly not to."

The assumption of active parenthood was new. Because the boys were in their twenties, though, little supervision was required. I let them be. I watched them make forays into the music business and helped whenever I could. The single strain was in my relationship with Jacques. He had kept his homosexuality a secret when he lived in St. Louis, but he became increasingly open about it once in Los Angeles. Until he moved into my home, we had never broached the topic, not that we ever had long discussions about sex. But now Jacques made no attempt to hide the fact that he dated men.

The strain came in Jacques's perception of my attitude toward homosexuality. He was convinced I disapproved. He thought I looked down on the lifestyle. I could never convince him that he misinterpreted my motives. When I warned him about his lifestyle, I referred to his promiscuity. I was wary of his companions. He'd pick up men in Hollywood, many of whom were hustlers, and have no compunction about bringing them back to the house. They'd be getting high in the den or lounging by the pool. My judgment might have been rash, but they seemed like riffraff to me. I believe my reaction would have been the same had Jacques been a heterosexual picking up female prostitutes. But my son didn't see it that way. He thought I was condemning him for being gay. I argued otherwise; I said that, having been in show business some thirty years, I knew and had befriended dozens of gay men. I would never have dreamed of excluding anyone from my home because of their sexual preference. In my heart, I harbored no bias. Which isn't to say I'm squeaky clean on the subject. I'm certainly capable of making a remark or telling a joke spoofing gays, just as I've directed humor at blacks, Jews, Catholics, Baptists. No matter how impassioned my protest, though, Jacques saw me and my admonitions as anti-gay.

I realize now—far more than I did twenty years ago when my sons came to live with me—that I'm not always the easiest man to talk to. I can see why Jacques took my reserve as disapproval. We had had a difficult history. I had, after all, abandoned him as an infant. My absence was long and, to his way of thinking, neglectful. For long periods of time, communication between me and Jacques was hit-and-miss. I didn't reach out as much as I could have. He didn't confide in me, nor I in him. His resentment seemed strong. And so was his ambition to make it as a singer—as strong as mine. The love I had for him was enormous, but I'm not sure I expressed it well. No matter what the explanation, we clashed.

"When Jacques went to L. A.," said his friend Jerome Davis, "he was making up for lost time. He did go a little wild—we all did in that period of our lives—but he also pursued his career seriously. Jacques's charisma grew and grew. His singing talent was tremendous, and it wasn't that many years later that he was performing in showcases around the city."

Jacques impressed everyone. He worked assiduously at his singing, and I have no doubt his talent in that area far exceeded mine. I regret I didn't help him more. My own career consumed me, especially during this period when Jacques was building his technique. But even if I had, for instance, taken off six months from my professional life and devoted myself to Jacques, I'm not sure Jacques would have accepted such attention, especially from me. But speculation is meaningless. The plain fact is that as the eighties progressed, Jacques went his way and I went mine.

In 1984, the occupants of my home included Kevin, Jacques, and a girlfriend of mine. *Benson* was still going full blast in its fifth successful season. I was fifty-six years old. I did not feel especially vulnerable. I had a steady girlfriend, my life was arranged the way I wanted it, and I felt in control. But I was not. Control is an illusion, a conceit, an extension of ego I was not smart enough to see. I found myself enchanted by a young lady who, like me, was romantically involved with someone else. Was I cautious? Was I reluctant? Was I wiser than I had been in my past relationships?

None of the above.

I plunged headlong into an affair that proved far more than an affair. This time I met a woman who not only changed my life but forced me to throw out the old handbook, the one that had been misguiding my romantic relationships ever since the lure of forbidden sex first brought my blood to a boil.

# Donna Brown Guillaume

"It was 1984, Jesse Jackson was running for president, and I was making strides in my career at CBS news. The last thing I was looking for was involvement with an older man. I was thirty-one, once married and divorced, and enjoying a good relationship with a guy who lived in New York. In fact, I was on the verge of being transferred to our New York office when I happen to schedule a lunch with a friend at Amagi, a Japanese restaurant on Sunset across from Gower Studios. My friend is late. Out of nowhere, here comes Robert Guillaume over to my table.

" 'Hello,' he says.

" 'Hello,' I reply.

" 'Are you alone?'

" 'Waiting for a friend. But you're welcome to wait with me.'

" 'I'd love to,' he explains, 'but I'm with some people.'

"Then he sits down and joins me until my friend arrives. Naturally I knew who he was. Everyone knew Benson. Beyond that, my older sister Candy is a great singer and actress who had appeared with him in *Purlie*.

" 'How come I never met you?' he asks. 'Didn't you see the show?'

" 'I was too busy doing homework. I was still in high school.'

"We continue to chat. This is a man of considerable charm. There's nothing I mention that doesn't interest him. The later my luncheon companion, the more he learns about me—my degree from Harvard in African American studies, my job as a producer for the KCBS TV show *Two on the Town*. I know his reputation as a player—my sister and Faye Hauser are good friends—but I'm nonetheless flattered by his attention. Beyond that, his conversation is nothing short of brilliant. After some twenty minutes, the encounter is over. *Nice meeting Robert Guillaume*, I think to myself, *he's a fascinating guy*. Later that afternoon, I'm on the phone with my boyfriend in New York, telling him who I met at lunch, when my assistant gives me a message—*Robert Guillaume is on the phone*. 'Look, I've got another call,' I tell my boyfriend. 'It's Guillaume, isn't it?' 'How did you know that?' 'I knew,' is all my boyfriend says. Robert wants to take me to dinner that night. I tell him I'm busy. What about lunch tomorrow? The man is hard to resist.

"We pick up where we left off the day before. The rapport is strong. Most men who are good talkers are not good listeners. Robert is both. I go through my history, how my father was one of the Tuskegee Airmen of World War II, how my family background had provided me strong stability, how the racial politics of the late sixties and early seventies radicalized me. My college years—from '69 to '73—molded me. I became a fiery activist. I was proud that, through our protest, Harvard divested its interest in oil companies supporting Portugal's colonies in Africa. We weren't the kind of black consciousness group that insisted fried chicken be served in the cafeteria; we had an international perspective. After graduation, I spent time in Cuba. As a result, my phone was tapped—and my parents' phone as well—proving the extent of our government's paranoia. In the Watergate era, I saw nothing but hypocrisy and malfeasance in America's domestic and foreign policy. When I went to work, I tried publishing in New York before moving to L. A., where I got into news. I had a nice little life, a little car, a little house in Silver Lake. When I started producing at *Two on the Town*, I interviewed a number of stars—Marlon Brando, Quincy Jones, Lionel Richie, Henry Mancini—so I was not especially impressed with Robert's celebrity. I was, however, impressed with his mind. And his openness to my ideas. He was clearly attracted to smart women—another unusual attribute for a man.

"We were drawn to one another sexually. The physical pull was powerful. We were both honest about our situations. I told him about my boyfriend in New York; he told me he was living with a woman. Our dating remained innocent for weeks—not through moral high-mindedness on our part, but because I'd contracted bronchitis. He'd come over my house and bring wonton soup, flowers, books by Alice Walker. He couldn't have been sweeter or more attentive. I was definitely falling. But how could it ever work out? I was about to be transferred to New York, where my boyfriend was waiting for me. Besides—no matter how brilliant or sweet this man might have been—he was twenty-five years older. It just wasn't meant to be. Or was it?

"Fate stepped in. The producer who was transferring me to New York got fired. Suddenly there was no New York job. My boyfriend urged me to come anyway. He sensed a switch in my attitude. But I still had my L. A. position and couldn't see myself moving back East without the assurance of work. And then there was Robert. Robert was becoming increasingly important. Some three or four weeks after we met, we became lovers. Our lovemaking was wonderful. Robert was wonderful. He'd come to my little place in Silver Lake. After we were together, he always spent the night—it was never love on the run. I wondered about this woman living in his home in Tarzana. 'I've had other dalliances before,' he explained. 'She understands.' It was hard for me to understand. Here was this big TV star, standing in my tiny bathroom, ringing out his drawers and hanging his T-shirt over my shower so he could have clean underwear the next day. Then he'd go off to work and shoot another *Benson*. It was strange, but it was also beautiful. In spite of the difference in age, the difference in our work, in spite of everything, we couldn't stay away from each other. I thrived on Robert's company. He said the same about me. Not that our compatibility was based upon like-mindedness. We argued books and theater and theology; we argued about everything under the sun. Robert is stimulated by spirited debate. He and I also have vastly different views of politics. My activism made him uneasy. He invited me to go with him to Israel, where he was entertaining. He had a fond view of the Holy Land. I did not. Because Israel was South Africa's number-one supplier of arms, I refused to set foot in the country. Anyone aiding the apartheid regime was no friend of mine. Robert was amazed and, I believe, impressed that I turned down the trip out of plain principle.

"In spite of the fact that I was falling deeply in love, I retained a bit of skepticism. There was the matter of Robert's reputation. Beyond his affinity for young women, there was the fact of his being an actor. I knew that actors don't always make the best mates. Their occupational hazards—especially the inevitable self-involvement—are considerable. I considered myself an enlightened woman, a feminist. Male actors from Robert's generation were not famous for embracing feminism. And yet I detected in his character a desire to understand exactly where I was coming from. I think he was attracted to me—at least in part—just because my ideas about male/female relationships were so new to him. I didn't want to give up my job. I didn't want to be kept. I didn't want to sacrifice my career for anyone. Nor was I willing to sacrifice my independence."

I was fascinated by Donna and pursued her with intense determination. She was among the smartest people I had ever met—man or woman. She was cultured, she was fiery, she was beautiful, she was young. Her idealism and uncompromising politics were refreshing. She kept me on my toes. Her perspective on Hollywood and its racist ways was right on. Her female liberation acted like an aphrodisiac on me. She was just what I wanted—a modern woman who challenged, even defeated, my outmoded notions of male superiority. I recognized the freshness—and correctness—of her thinking. And beyond all that, she was sweetly charming and enticingly sexy.

When I met Donna, my relationship with Faye had been over for four years, but I don't believe I had fully recovered. There had been

other women since our debacle. But no one—not until Donna—
touched my heart like Faye. I realized that I had blown it with Faye.
I had messed up the vast majority of my relationships with women.
For a man who valued—and strived for—success, I was spectacularly
unsuccessful in this vital area. When Donna came along, I had to
think long and hard about how *not* to mess this one up.

"I kept my job," said Donna. "I kept my place. The last thing in the
world I wanted was dependence upon Robert. We had met in January,
and by summer things started changing. He asked his old girlfriend
to move out and asked me to move in. I moved in. It was me, Robert,
Kevin, and Jacques. His sons were cool. The vibe was good. Robert
liked me to travel with him, and sometime that summer we were in
Miami when he introduced me as his fiancée. Well, that was news to
me. I didn't know if he was serious or whether that was his usual way
of legitimizing his female companions to the world. A little later, I
asked him about it. He hemmed and hawed. I said it straight up. 'I
don't want to be "Robert Guillaume's next girlfriend." You're either
willing to make a commitment or not. If not, I understand. It's been
grand, but so long. I'll move out, find myself another place, get on
with my life. No hurt feelings, no regrets.' Robert listened long and
hard. That December, a year after we met, he filed a motion to divorce
Marlene."

It must sound strange. I'd been married to Marlene for thirty years,
but we'd been together for less than three. I respected the way she had
raised our sons. I respected her as a person. And yet contact between
us had been minimal. To see her was to remind myself of my negligence. Beyond that, I realized the reason I'd never divorced was fear—
fear of further commitment. My marriage was a safety net, a crutch,
an avoidance mechanism. It was silly. Yet, when I thought I might
lose Donna, I agonized over the decision. Maybe it was the Catholic
in me, maybe the coward in me. Maybe both. Or neither. Either way,

I was—and am—a creature of habit. I had operated my entire adult life on the premise that one marriage was enough. A second would only complicate my life—not to mention my finances. It took Donna Brown to shake me from my complacency. I did not want to lose this woman. But if I married her, I would be changing my life—and throwing out the old handbook. The idea both alarmed and excited me. I took the plunge.

Marlene was not necessarily heartened by the news. Like me, she had grown accustomed to our peculiar arrangement. Finally, though, the legalities went through and Donna and I were set to be married in September of 1985.

"Before I met Donna," said my daughter Pat, "I didn't quite know what to expect. After all, my father was marrying someone years younger than me. But it only took a few minutes for me to see that Donna had all the attributes I wanted in a sibling. She was warm and compassionate and determined to bond with everyone in Dad's extended family—no easy task. She's technically my stepmother, but emotionally we've become sisters."

A few months before the marriage, I sold my house in Tarzana. I wanted a fresh start with Donna, a new environment, one free of memories. Jacques and Kevin were ready to get places of their own— and I was ready to be alone with Donna. We stayed in the San Fernando Valley and found a home on Longridge Avenue in Sherman Oaks. The house had a tennis court, an indulgence to which I felt entitled. This was the year, after all, that I won an Emmy for *Benson.* Looking back, I recognize it as the year that found me at the top of my game. I saw my marriage as the start of a bright new chapter. My future was with Donna, and, once I made up my mind to embrace the notion of monogamy, I was overwhelmed by a feeling of calm certainty. *At long last, Guillaume, you're doing the right thing.*

⌒

"I knew the wedding was going to be special," said Carol Tillery Banks. "It was a small home wedding, with no more than twenty guests, in the lovely backyard of their new home on Longridge. Diane Watson, the California state senator who'd been Donna's fifth-grade teacher, on Okinawa of all places, officiated. I'd been divorced from Ron O'Neal for five years. Ron had left Hollywood and was hard to find, but we talked now and then. I made it a point to let him know that Bob wanted him there. Whatever Ron's personal problems might have been, Bob loved him dearly. But Ron was reluctant to attend. His self-esteem was suffering. 'If you don't come to this wedding,' I told him, 'I'll never speak to you again.' He knew I meant it. Well, the wedding was just about under way when Ron strolled into the backyard, dressed to the nines, looking like the movie star he once had been. Bob beamed from ear to ear. The men embraced. It was a shining moment. Two brothers, two supertalented actors whose careers had gone in such divergent directions. Their common road led back to Karamu. But the road ahead was unknown."

# Be Careful What You Wish For

It seemed like a ridiculous cliché. My wish was for freedom—the more the merrier. Why should care be required? How could one have too much freedom, especially in the area about which I cared so passionately—my acting? *Benson* had a seven-year run. In the sixth year, ABC put it up against *Dallas,* and the handwriting was on the wall. Before it was over, though, we'd produce some 158 episodes. I never tired of the character. He had an idiosyncratic spunk that kept him fresh. The tension in his life—between resentment and ambition, sarcasm and sweetness, cynicism and sincerity—struck the right balance for me. I saw the man for who he was.

I could also see a day when the camera would have no use for Benson—or for me. That's why I tried to develop other ways to express my artistry and, at the same time, make decent money. I directed and starred in a TV movie, *John Grin's Christmas,* a takeoff on Dickens's *A Christmas Carol* shot in Chicago. I played Scrooge. The experience was not especially edifying. I entertained on a cruise ship going to Norway and worked up a show that played Tahoe and Vegas, employing my perfect-pitch sons, Kevin and Jacques, as backup singers. My forays into nightclubs, though, were lackluster. I was never particularly comfortable or convincing. I was too stiff. That same stiffness probably contributed to my failure as a stand-up comic. At one point, I traveled to Red Deer, Canada, to try out a comedy act written by the illustrious Hal Kantor, the same man who had cast me in *Julia,* my first TV appearance back in the sixties. There was nothing wrong with Kantor's one-liners; there was everything wrong with my awkward delivery. I drew an audience because of *Benson*. But the poor Canadians who had braved the snow in hopes of a few good laughs left dejected. "The son-of-a-bitch," I heard one disgruntled patron mumble, "just ain't funny."

What worked for me on TV didn't seem to work live. I had learned to relax in that least relaxing of all theatrical environments—the TV studio. But stand-up requires sparkle, self-generating energy, nonstop whirls of wit. Cosby is stand-up. Pryor is stand-up. Redd Foxx, Moms Mabley, Flip Wilson, Slappy White. These are chatty, loose, lively, freewheeling, and genuinely funny people, on camera and off. It took cold-ass Canada to show me I lacked those skills.

Naturally, the failure was disappointing. But because I'd never aspired to comic greatness, I wasn't especially wounded. I recognized my limitations. My singing was a different matter; I had greater vanity. I had never quite given up the dream of making it as a vocalist. My voice was still intact. But I was still vexed by falling between the categorical cracks. I wasn't opera, but neither was I Top 40. I sure as hell wasn't Wayne Newton or Neil Diamond. My success as a singer had come solely in the context of musicals. No such roles were being offered. I tried like hell to make the transition from singing actor to solo singer, but only with marginal success. I never developed a following or got anything more than an isolated gig.

Clearly, TV was my bread and butter. On TV I had broken through from supporting to lead actor, and it was in TV programs that people found me most sympathetic. Benson had a depth that surprised even me. I was once flying first class from L. A. to New York when I noticed a man—a big beefy redneck—who had come out of the coach section and was staring at me. When he finally approached me, I thought, *Oh shit, what the fuck is this going to be?* " 'Scuse me," he said, "but ain't you that boy that plays Benson?" "Yes," I replied, ignoring the "boy." "Remember that episode when your mother dies?" he asked. "Yes," I repeated, wondering where this was leading. "Well, my mother died under similar circumstances. Never could accept her death till I saw how you treated it on your show. Just wanna thank ya'." What I had assumed would be an assault was, in reality, an appreciation. Over the years I've had hundreds of letters from people who addressed Benson as a personal friend. Latchkey kids, especially those who watched the daily reruns, were filled with gratitude. "You were there for me every day," wrote one girl. "You made me laugh. You didn't care whether I had a lisp or a bad complexion. You kept me from being lonely. Thank you, Benson, for making me feel good."

Benson had gone from butler and cook to lieutenant governor. One could imagine him becoming the governor himself. He had cunningly worked the system and prospered. I saw him as a metaphor for blacks in America, a guy with the gutsy determination and smarts to better himself in spite of the bullshit surrounding him. I saw him as a metaphor for all people looking to improve their station in life. I was proud of Benson. Now I wanted to do something different.

Though I've never viewed emotional intimacy as my forte, the TV sitcom demanded more intimacy from me than did any other form. I became comfortable in the closed set and the tight three-act structure. Because I thrive on work, the nonstop routine—show after show, week after week—suited me. TV was clearly my medium. TV also afforded me what seemed like my best shot at absolute freedom— a show that I could develop according to my own ideas. With that in mind, and with the backing of my loyal manager, Phil Margo, I conceived the idea of *The Robert Guillaume Show*, the logical—and, I thought, daring—next step after *Benson*.

The planning began in 1987. Donna became pregnant in 1988. ABC committed to a pilot and twelve subsequent shows. Cosby, of course, was the megastar of TV in the eighties. I have tremendous admiration for Bill. When NBC put his all-black family show on the air, they pitted it against Tom Selleck's *Magnum P.I.*, the top-rated show of the season. At first, it looked like the lamb being led to slaughter.

But six weeks later, *Magnum* was missing in action. Cosby was sitting atop the world. Bill's coup was nothing short of spectacular. He understood that America—white as well as black—was ready to see an African American family in which both parents were prosperous professionals. He infused that domestic situation with wit and charm. The Huxtables won our hearts, and the show ran from 1984 through 1992. It was in the middle of that run that *The Robert Guillaume Show* made its debut.

I didn't want to do what Cosby had done—mainly because Bill had already done it. I wanted a family situation, but one with racial complexity. I saw my character, Edward Sawyer, as a psychologist, a single father with two kids. I gave him a father, played by Hank Rolike, a proud, retired Pullman porter who'd saved his pennies for his son's education. I knew many such men and had certainly fantasized about having such a father myself. The romantic setup was simple: Edward falls for a white woman who also has a child. The woman, played by Wendy Phillips, is sympathetic and intelligent. She and Edward struggle with the misunderstandings—some comic, some serious—that inevitably accompany interracial romance. In my view, these issues had never before been addressed on network TV, certainly not in the context of a sitcom. The notion excited and challenged me. It also almost destroyed my marriage.

"Had I not been pregnant," Donna said, "I would have left Robert over that show. His attitude infuriated me. He was intransigent about his position, and I was just as adamant about mine. I knew he was wrong. We argued for months, and the arguments got ugly. We screamed and shouted and slammed doors. The rancor went on for the entire duration—all thirteen shows. I was vehemently, violently, passionately opposed to an interracial relationship for his TV character. I tried to be reasonable. I tried imagining what it was like growing up as a black man in St. Louis in the thirties. You're told you're not worthy of anything. You can't even look at a white woman, much less touch one. I further understood that if you attain a certain success, the one thing you want to stick back in the white man's face is your dating a white woman. *Look what I got—and there's not shit you can do about it.* I knew that attitude had an emotional base, but in the real world of American TV, it made absolutely no sense. If anything, it was self-destructive. The bottom line was clear: black women didn't want to see it; white men didn't want to see it; and, of course, white men ran the network. Finally the network didn't want to see it either.

"Robert insisted he didn't want to copy Cosby. But it was Robert who allowed his daughter, Melissa, to stay up a half hour later on Thursday nights to watch *The Cosby Show,* just because it was the only black family comedy—and one that provided healthy role models for black kids. Surely there was room for another all-black family in the all-white sea of network TV. In the name of boldness, Robert refused to listen. To my mind, his position made no more sense than picking up a gun and shooting himself in the foot."

Our fights became vituperative. Donna wouldn't relent. I argued she was overanalyzing my motives; I saw this as merely an attempt to intelligently frame a situation that I thought millions of viewers would find fascinating—and funny. I took the story seriously, but I also knew it was just that—a story. The story, though, if rendered with sensitivity, could make television history. After the success of *Benson,* I was looking for a breakthrough. It had nothing to do with my wanting a white woman or in, more generally, black men wanting white women. My aim was to create a small but sweet story in which two sympathetic people try to bridge a gap of racial misunderstanding. We like them; we root for them; we hope they make it. Along the way, they stumble, say funny things, find themselves in funny dilemmas, allow their essential goodness to lead them to a kind of romantic enlightenment. Donna could see none of this through her fury. She reacted in a way I would have never anticipated.

"Robert's reaction to my objections," she remembered, "came down to, 'I'm the star of the show, I'll do what I want.' As his wife and partner in life, I thought I had a say-so in something this important. He didn't. He went his own way. The network warned him to take the black/white romance slowly. The public, they claimed, needed time to get used to it. Wisely, he took eight episodes before he and Ann kiss. But then—out of nowhere—ABC ran the shows out of sequence, undermining their own admonition. The second night the show aired, he had his tongue down this woman's throat. The network didn't want to support *The Robert Guillaume Show;* in fact, they deliberately sabotaged it. Thirteen episodes were shot, and that was it. The show bombed. Robert would never have another opportunity of that kind again. He blew it."

There's no doubt that Donna was right. My experiment failed. In retrospect, it's clear I overplayed my hand. Hollywood wasn't ready. America wasn't ready. And on top of that, the show probably just wasn't funny enough. I was up against black women who thought Benson—because to them I was still Benson—should have a black wife. I was up against white men who were uncomfortable with miscegenation. Donna had seen all this coming. I had not. I'm the kind of son-of-a-bitch who grabs hold of something and doesn't let go. I had it all reasoned out. I kept telling myself that the only reason I got into acting was the freedom it afforded. Now I wanted to extend that freedom to designing my own drama. The bulldog in me would not be restrained. Donna's argument fell on deaf ears. I pulled out my ace—"I'm the boss"—and placed it on the table. Then the table collapsed.

A month or two after that collapse I lacked the perspective I have today. I was still convinced my plan had merit. I was willing to take the blame but would not admit to regrets. Pride is a motherfucker. My pride was intense. I shook off the defeat and looked for other work. I was fortunate to find a good part in *Lean on Me,* the film starring Morgan Freeman. Morgan played Joe Clark, the legendary tough-as-nails high school principal. I played his supervisor. I had one scene I cherish. In it Morgan and I are at each other's throats. We're really fuming. I get the last word. With unchecked conviction, I get to exclaim, "I'm the head nigger around here." Then I turn to him and add a line that is not in the script—"Now let's have lunch."

Making up with Donna was not easy. Our marriage had been wounded. She was hurt by my refusal to heed her advice, and I was alarmed by her interference in my work. Our daughter, Rachel, was born at the end of 1988, a time when her parents' relationship was at risk. We adored the child and realized the damage a divorce would do to her. Moreover, we had just started our family. Donna was the woman I wanted. After a lifetime of failed arrangements, this one was supposed to work—and put an end to my restless discontent. I respected Donna's ability to embrace all the members of my disparate family. She maintained a good relationship with Patricia, Melissa's mother, thus insuring that Rachel and Melissa would share a close sisterhood. Donna was also kind to my sons and their mother, Marlene. Her warm and generous sense of family further motivated me to make our marriage work, as did the knowledge that her wonderful parents, Vera and Larry Brown, had been married for forty-six years.

It wasn't easy. I thought it would just be a matter of throwing out the old handbook with its chauvinistic codes. But the handbook was imprinted on my brain. Something about teaching old dogs new tricks. When Rachel was born, I was sixty-one. In theory, I accepted the tenets of the New Woman. In theory, who could argue with the principle of equality between men and women? In theory, sexism exists on the same abject level as racism. But theoretical idealism and day-to-day reality can clash. As an abstraction, the liberated woman was a tantalizing notion. But when that woman, in the person of Donna, got involved in my work life, I balked. Especially when our outlooks differed so sharply. When her outlook proved more perceptive than mine, though, I had to reexamine. I argued, for example, that if *The Robert Guillaume Show* had made Donna unhappy, that had not been my intent. Her happiness, I contended, should not be dependent upon my artistic endeavors. Out of this painful episode, though, I realized something I had never seen before—I excluded women from the major decisions in my life. I might have heard their opinions, but I felt free to disregard them. If I were to stay with Donna, this regulation from the old handbook—*I'll do whatever I want to do whenever I want to do it*—required radical revision.

Before that revision could take full effect, however, a dire circumstance diverted my attention. I was not prepared for such a tragic turn of events. It was one thing to lose a grandmother or a mother; it was another to lose a son.

# "He Was Broken for Me"

The song was recorded in 1983 for Savoy Records by James Cleveland and the Los Angeles Gospel Messengers. The soloist is my son, listed in the credits as Jacques Williams. The lyric refers to the Crucifixion. "He's set me free," sings Jacques, "from the power of sin and disease." The style is high soul. Jacques's technique is remarkable, his voice an instrument of tremendous feeling and subtle grace. This is, after all, a highly challenging form of vocalizing that very few—among them, Sam Cooke, Aretha Franklin, Al Green—ever master. At a young age, Jacques was on his way. He went to Reverend Cleveland's church, I believe, motivated more by music than religion. Cleveland, called the King of Gospel, was recognized as a giant in the field. A great singer, composer, and vocal arranger, he was a magnet for aspiring vocalists. Cleveland was also a homosexual who populated his choir with many gay men. The gay tradition in black gospel singing is a long and distinguished one.

Cleveland provided one half of Jacques's musical training, Phil Moore, the gifted arranger and vocal coach, the other. If Cleveland represented black soul, Phil symbolized black show business. It was a glorious combination. Jacques had selected the perfect teachers, and, as the eighties progressed, his talent blossomed.

"I moved to Los Angeles in 1986," remembered Jerome Davis, "and lived with Jacques in Burbank. He was working at Hollywood Sheet Music and getting his showcase together. Jacques pursued his career with real dedication. He was organized—his cassettes were alphabetized, his mailing list always updated—and never failed to fill a room when he was singing. There are hundreds of aspiring vocalists in L. A., but none were more diligent or charismatic than Jacques. He was on his way. He felt his father's disapproval—he told me that—but that only served to motivate him more."

"Jacques and I were close," said Carol Tillery Banks, "and we spoke often. He was industrious in much the same way as his dad. He didn't feel as though Bob accepted him—or even cared about him—but deep down Jacques knew better. Bob isn't the easiest guy in the world to talk to. He can be moody, and he's not always the same. If you catch Bob on a good day, you'll have a sympathetic ear. On a bad day, he can be distant. Jacques was prone to misinterpret his father's moods. Jacques was also never one to patronize. Like his father, he was not an ass-kisser. Jacques was all about integrity.

"To his credit, Bob sought to understand the why of his son's homosexuality. When I brought him evidence that sexual inclinations are genetic and not arbitrary, Bob was relieved. I remember Jacques telling me that, if given a choice, he would not choose to be gay. 'Being both black and gay,' he said, 'is too much.' But he was both, and he came to accept himself with a degree of serenity."

"Jacques was a people person," said Donna. "He was a wonderful guy and much loved by the world. He sparkled. We were good friends, and it was difficult to see the distance between him and Robert. I've never detected even a glimmer of homophobia in Robert. But that doesn't mean that he wasn't disappointed that Jacques was gay. Most straight fathers—if they're honest—want straight sons. If your son is gay, you'll have a relationship, but it's inevitably going to be different from the one you imagined. That requires an adjustment in thinking. Robert made that adjustment, but unfortunately Jacques didn't feel it. He harbored resentments about what he considered his dad's neglect. The gap was never bridged."

When AIDS became a public health issue, my concern for Jacques turned to alarm. Jacques mistook that for prejudice. I worried that he lacked an adequate sense of self-protection, that he was unable to discriminate between who was good for him and who was not. Looking back, I see I made several mistakes. I never adequately expressed my admiration for his talent. I made positive statements but with insufficient enthusiasm. Telling people I admire them—or, for that matter, expressing gratitude—doesn't come naturally. Unlike me, Jacques was extremely down-to-earth. He was without pretense and did not, as I often did, use intelligence like a sword. We were so different and yet so alike that it's no wonder our emotional connection was tenuous.

"We were all worried about Jacques," said Kevin, "but no one said anything. Then in 1988, he and I were extras on *The Robert Guillaume Show*. Jacques was wearing a turtleneck, and when he took it off I saw something that looked like a rash. Or a lesion. I asked him about it. His answer was vague, and I didn't push him. I knew my brother. He was a private guy. I left him alone, but my heart was hammering. I was frightened for him. We all were.

"The news came between Thanksgiving and Christmas of that year. Dad called. 'Your brother is sick,' is all he said. I was leaving for St. Louis the next day. When I returned, Mom came back with me. She stayed to care for Jacques."

"Bob was determined that Jacques be surrounded by family," remembered Carol Tillery Banks. "He brought out Jacques's mother, Marlene, who made a permanent move to be with her son."

"Dad brought me out to California as well," said Pat. "He knew Jacques and I were close and wanted me with him as much as possible. In the last years of his life, there was something clearly self-destructive about Jacques's behavior. Before he could change that behavior, though, it was too late. He had the HIV virus, which would, over the next year, develop into full-blown AIDS."

My own reaction was one of helplessness and horror. We provided whatever care was necessary. Family and friends rallied around. But there was no hiding the truth. Dozens of calls to dozens of doctors yielded the same prognosis, the worst-case scenario, no cure. These were the dark years when, like the plague, AIDS devastated whole segments of the community. In James Cleveland's church, where Jacques had gained prominence, the disease took a terrible toll. Cleveland himself would succumb in 1991. For two long years, we dealt with the situation as best we could. It was a time when Jacques's character was tested. He passed with flying colors. He remained steady and brave. His essential kindness never wavered. He comforted us rather than we him. We hoped against hope that he'd hold on.

After the debacle of *Guillaume,* my career was in limbo. *Lean on Me* was fine, but then my phone went dead. With my new marriage tottering and my son ailing, staying at home was the last thing I wanted to do. My preference has always been to work. Work is my refuge and my raison d'être. When Donna and I saw Andrew Lloyd Webber's *Phantom of the Opera* in New York, she said, "You could play the Phantom." I agreed. The part had enormous appeal to me for reasons both practical and emotional. The role required a certain athleticism; even more, it demanded an actor/singer with an operatic lilt and a tragic facade. Psychologically, I identified with a protagonist who slips through life hiding behind a mask. I was intrigued. I saw the musical several times and became even more convinced that I had the requisite skills to carry the show.

I was particularly motivated because of the failure of *Guillaume.* To keep my profile high (in fact, to avoid oblivion), I knew I'd have to fight. I had my agents make calls. I made calls myself. The producers were interested. Auditions were arranged. I mastered the material and gave an effective reading. My voice was still strong and the melodies much to my liking. I flew to New York to audition for Hal Prince, director of the original cast. All he said was, "Thank you, Robert." I went back to California without a clue. The plane ride seemed especially long. Before I reached home, Prince's office had called with a four-word message: "You're the new Phantom." With a sigh of relief, I realized my career had been given new life.

Something about the Phantom spoke to my soul. Maybe it was his smoldering subtexts—his lack of recognition, his unrealized ambition, his thwarted love—that resonated so powerfully. I liked the antiheroic nature of the character. He's a dashing demon with heart. It was exciting to wear the cape and thrilling to don the makeup. Controversy ensued. Some thought it inappropriate for an African American to play the part. Others thought it especially appropriate. For me, the Phantom is estranged from society, just as blacks are estranged. He—and we—are the ultimate outsiders. Reviewers saw it my way and were enthusiastic. Box office was strong. We opened in May of 1990 at the Ahmanson in downtown Los Angeles. Jacques was in the audience.

I was overjoyed to see him. He was thin and weak, but his spirit was intact. When we embraced, I could feel his bones. His frailty distressed me, but I hid my concern. I went on with the show over the next months, but Jacques was always on my mind. I visited him often. His spiritual energy never waned, but his body was failing. The deterioration was appalling to all of us who loved him. On stage, I put those anxieties into the character of the Phantom, a man at odds with his ego. The Phantom yearns for recognition just as he avoids it. His white mask sits upon his black face. His murderous rage against the world and its injustices is channeled into songs of frustration and beauty. He is agonized. My own agony deepened when, in the middle of the run, I developed an excruciating case of shingles. Marlene developed shingles at the same time. It was as if we had both translated our anguish into physical pain.

"The eight months that Robert played 'Phantom,'" said Donna, "was also a low point for our marriage. As Robert told an interviewer, he was either preparing for the gig, doing the gig, or recovering from the gig. I had an infant to care for. I argued that we should have live-in help, but Robert didn't want a stranger in the house. He felt that, down the line, I'd regret having someone being closer to Rachel than myself. I didn't see it that way. The truth is that I didn't see much of Robert at all. I was proud of his performance and gratified that it was a success. Andrew Lloyd Webber called Robert 'fantastic' and said, 'You are the Phantom as I envisioned him to be.' I saw the show at least twenty times. But I also saw our relationship suffering. Each night his dressing room was crowded with everyone from Quincy Jones to Sidney Poitier. All of Hollywood wanted to see him in this role. He wouldn't arrive home until two or three in the morning. I understood his attitude. He was gratified that people who knew him only as Benson could now appreciate the range of his acting as well as musical talent. Having three thousand people leaping to their feet, giving him a standing ovation night after night did wonders for him. But that applause didn't do much to relieve my loneliness and sense of being trapped.

"We agreed that we needed to escape alone for a long weekend. After a Sunday matinee we were set to leave for Laguna Beach. The theater was dark Monday, so we'd have at least thirty-six hours to ourselves. After the performance, it seemed like the whole world had descended on Robert's dressing room for autographs. I mean, there was a mob. I whispered in his ear, 'Why not excuse yourself? Just say, "Thanks, but I've a pressing engagement"—and leave.' He refused. Said that his fans had made him. Said he didn't want to appear rude. Fuming, I went out to the limo and waited for what seemed forever. When he finally arrived, we both exploded. I screamed, 'Why, at least this one time, couldn't you choose me over them?' He screamed, 'I thought I'd married a woman who understood the obligations of an actor!' The screaming escalated until we both finally fell into silence. We made our getaway, but it was a joyless day down in Laguna. We wanted nothing to do with each other. I was convinced he didn't understand me, and he was certain I didn't understand him. The demands of his career took their toll on our marriage."

⟶

"At the end," said Jacques's cousin Carla, "Jacques was a stick figure. Physically, he became another person. I hardly recognized him. Jacques was someone who did everything for himself. Now he could do nothing. He was bedridden and couldn't lift himself up, couldn't walk to the bathroom, couldn't reach for a glass of water. We did it all for him. He became our infant child."

"His mother and I and so many of his friends," remembered Pat, "stayed by his side. There was a certain serenity to his soul that shined through. Despite the terrible pain, he continued to give and receive love."

"Reverend Carl Bean, a minister from a gay church," said Jerome Davis, "came to give last rites. I sat on the bed next to him. I said, 'If you hear me, Jacques, squeeze my hand. Know that we all love you. Know that love never dies.' The pressure was slight, but it was undeniable. Jacques heard."

"Jacques's bravery in the face of certain death," stated Reverend Bill Minson, a friend to me and my family, "never wavered. I was there during his last hours. In his eyes, I didn't see fear, but acceptance. He was at peace. That same night I was with Robert before his performance. The theater was sold out. I wondered if Robert could go on. I know I couldn't have done it. But Robert did—out of respect to his profession, and out of respect to his son."

Jacques died December 23, 1990. He was thirty-two. At his memorial service, singers Carl Anderson and Dianne Reeves, his friends and colleagues, sang movingly. His brother, Kevin, spoke eloquently. The ministers Bill Minson and Carl Bean eulogized his beautiful spirit. I, for whom words come so easily, could not speak. Along with his mother and sisters, his brother and friends, Donna and I wept. The mourning began. The mourning without end.

# "This Is the Moment"

I forged ahead, devoting inordinate time and energy to the recording of a CD, *This Is the Moment.* I did songs—"Beauty and the Beast," "The Circle of Life," "The Phantom of the Opera"— from contemporary musicals. My producer, Beau Ray Fleming, and my arranger, Gene Page, were enormously talented and unwaveringly supportive. They were convinced that, after my success in *Phantom*, I'd have a chance at cracking the music game. I thought I had a shot at realizing my longtime goal—to sell my voice to a mass market. I was wrong. Musically, the disc turned out fine. Commercially, it didn't make a dent. Nor did another record I made, *As Time Goes By,* with producer John Benton. Both were time-consuming projects that never found an audience. In retrospect, I can't help but castigate myself. Late at night, when I can't sleep and melodies echo through my head, I hear a voice saying, "Guillaume, you goddamn fool, if you'd put all this concentration into Jacques's singing career—and not your own—you'd be better off. You backed the wrong horse." But I was an egotist, and I did what I did. Could have, should have, would have . . . it made no difference.

My television career got a minor boost in 1991 when I was cast as a detective on an NBC series, *Pacific Station.* After thirteen episodes, though, the show folded, and I began to flounder. I did some voice-overs and commercials, easy work but hardly high drama. Then someone at one of the networks envisioned *Driving Miss Daisy* as a major TV series and cast me in the Morgan Freeman role. Joan Plowright was set to be Miss Daisy. The problems were many. The scripts were written in a dialogue I found offensive. It was a blatant case of well-intentioned white people trying to render what they consider folksy black talk. Folksy was downright insulting. I felt pressured to "spook up" the character and flatly refused. When we finally shot the pilot, I ignored their language and injected my own. It all proved an exercise in futility. Minutes after the taping had stopped, the verdict came in for the Rodney King case, and the L. A. riots erupted. In the light of the events of 1992, this curious relationship between a white woman and her black driver seemed irrelevant. The show was scrapped, and I was relieved.

In continuing to do what actors are obliged to do—pursue work—I discovered that people were far more impressed with me than I was with myself. They figured that because I'd been a TV star, I wouldn't accept lesser roles. That wasn't true. Before *Benson* and after, I saw myself as an actor for hire—plain and simple. If you had a decent role, I'd play it. If you offered a decent wage, I'd take it. Hardheaded to the end, I also wouldn't give up on my musical career. When an opportunity arose to play Cyrano de Bergerac in a Broadway musical, I grabbed it. Unfortunately, the production, book, and score were less than stellar. The show opened and closed in the blink of an eye. I had far greater success as an animated character. When Disney called about *The Lion King,* my pride led me to assume that I was to play the lion. Instead they wanted me for the monkey, Rafiki. "Why," I asked my agent indignantly, "must a black man always play the monkey? Who's playing the King?" James Earl Jones, I was told. "Fine," I said, "I'll play the monkey."

In the early nineties, there was more movement in my marriage than my career. Donna insisted that we go into therapy together. I'm no fan of therapy, but I went.

When I say I'm no fan of therapy, I mean the kind of therapy to which I've been exposed. That was essentially marriage counseling. My expectation was that if the therapist saw patterns in my behavior that made me stumble, those patterns would be pointed out. Instead, the therapist allowed us to say whatever we liked and, from that, expected us to draw our own conclusions. My view might have been midwestern and hopelessly provincial; I may well have missed the whole point; but, for my money, if you go to a doctor, you want a prescription. You want concrete advice and clear direction. You want to be told how to get better. I learned no such thing. My behavior in the therapist's office was largely an exercise in self-control. I wanted my marriage to endure, so I fulfilled my wife's request. I tried. But as a psychological process, I found it an exercise in futility.

We did, however, agree not to fight in front of Rachel. With an occasional slip, we've kept that agreement. Despite my resistance to therapy, I hung in. And despite my inclination to cling to the old handbook, I finally threw it out. To keep my family together, I changed my ancient attitudes about women. The business about being Lord of the Castle had to go. A tendency to dominate is not easy to abandon, especially for a man well into his sixties. I approached the problem from two directions. The first was purely intellectual. I reasoned that there is no greater moral justification for a male to exert power over a female than there is for a white to rule a black. Second, I saw that my peace of my mind depended upon a major adjustment in attitude. I'd made messes of all my romantic relationships and was determined to avoid another failure. I could continue to try to control my wife, or I could try to be happy. Those were the choices. I opted for the latter.

"I also saw that I had to stop living with the notion," said Donna, "of always having one foot out the door. When things got shaky in our marriage, the first thing I'd say was, 'I'm gone.' I did that for too many years. The day I gave up that idea and recommitted to Robert was the day I found greater peace of mind. I realized I didn't want to leave Robert; I didn't want a bifurcated family; I wanted a united family and was willing to do whatever it took. Actually, work helped enormously.

"I exec produced a TV movie about black cinema, *You Must Remember This,* starring Robert, Tim Reid, Roscoe Lee Browne, and Brock Peters. Later I developed *Happily Ever After,* a cartoon series of multiethnic fairy tales that aired on HBO for three seasons. We shot thirty-nine shows, all of which featured Robert's voice as the narrator. We captured a large audience, won industry awards, and accomplished our goals—to retell fairy tales to which kids of different ethnic groups could relate."

Donna's success as a producer didn't surprise me. I had always known she was gifted. What did surprise me, though, was my increasing ability to give up control—and let her have it. She was the producer, I was the actor, and that was fine. In a professional arena, I could live with her being the boss. She headed our production company and pushed my career. In our personal life, I could live with her being my equal. All that represented a dramatic evolution in my attitude. The evolution was not entirely smooth.

My health became an issue. In 1996, I was attending the funeral of my friend Margaux Hemingway. During the service, I collapsed. Unconscious, I had to be rushed to the hospital. The prognosis was ambiguous, but a pacemaker was installed. Not long afterward, I suffered a TIA—transient ischemic attack—resulting in a brief slurring of words and slight drooping of my mouth muscles. The symptoms went away. Later I learned if you have a TIA, you're likely to have a stroke. At the time, though, my doctors issued no warnings. But I knew physical deterioration had set in. I would never quite be the same again.

Sexually, I was slowing down. This is nothing a man wants to admit. At least this man. Sex is the life force, the driving impetus. Sex had been my strength—and my weakness. Either way, powerful sexuality had been my steady companion since I was boy. When it began to wane, even slightly, I felt the loss. I always assumed I'd be like one of those patriarchs from the Old Testament, full tilt to the end. I don't say I've entirely enjoyed the quietude, but it has had certain benefits I would have never imagined. Calmness can be cool.

When I married Donna, I didn't think twice about our age gap. I saw myself as Peter Pan. Younger women had long been my preference, some might say my obsession. Karin was nine years younger, Faye more than twenty years my junior. Well, it's one thing when you're fifty-seven and your lady is thirty-two. But it's quite another when you're seventy and she's forty-five. Allowances must be made. Making those allowances was emotionally painful, but I saw them as necessary. I also saw intimacy in a new light. Our sexual parts do not promote genuine intimacy. For many—including me—they often give the false impression of intimacy. When those parts lose intensity, you're forced to face the true meaning of intimacy. Whom do you really want to be with? Comfort, understanding, and compassion take on tremendous importance. Your perspective changes. Slowly, I was changing. I was feeling enormous gratitude to Donna, not only for the quality of her heart and mind, but for the love she offered me and my extended family. She also made certain I was involved with Rachel's life. While Donna was at the office and I was home between gigs, I'd drive Rachel to school, take her to the doctor and dentist. Donna and I attended parent/teacher conferences together, a new and satisfying activity for me. Never before had I had the time— or taken the time—to be a hands-on parent. Rachel is a bright and beautiful girl and I cherish every day I spend with her.

Things were looking up in 1998 when producer Aaron Sorkin put me in *Sports Night*, a network television show about a network television show on which I portrayed Isaac Jaffee, the exec producer of the show, who views the fray from a distance. It was the best part I had had in years. Jaffee is the link to the network bosses, the éminence grise and patriarch to a staff of young writers, researchers, and on-air talent. I liked playing the wise old man. I liked being Father Confessor. I related to Jaffee, who'd earned his stripes as a workaday journalist. His ascension in TV bureaucracy was based on skill and integrity. He was a wily survivor—tough but caring. The show itself was cutting edge, the banter quick, the characters quirky, the situations smart.

The lessons I had learned about television acting were brought to bear. I never felt more relaxed. I was able to let the camera watch me. What seems so simple had taken me a lifetime to learn. To allow the camera to come to me—rather than pursuing it—is a Zenlike blessing. Few actors realize the power of restraint. There's the scene, for instance, in *Glengarry Glen Ross* in which Jack Lemmon is verbally decimated by Alec Baldwin. Lemmon says nothing; he simply lets the camera record the desolation in his eyes. It's one of the most moving moments in film. *Here I am,* Lemmon silently says to the camera, *Come get me.*

The first season of *Sports Night* was a success. Camaraderie among the writers and cast was good, the ratings solid, and my visibility high. It was great being back on network TV. The show had a buzz, and my career received a much-needed boost. Then during the second season, on a sunny morning in January, my life, as I had known it for seventy-one years, suddenly came to a screeching halt.

# Stroke of Fate

*I'm inside a dark tunnel. I don't know how the hell I got here, but I can't get out. Can't get my body to do what I want it to do. I give orders to my left arm*—Move, you fucker!—*but my left arm doesn't move. Tell my left leg to move, but it won't budge. The connection between thought and action is broken. The agony is more than physical; it's emotional. I'm filled with frustration. And fear. Fear overwhelms me. Fear in a thousand forms. A kind of fear I've never known before.*

They called it a stroke. I prefer to call it a brain attack. My operating system fell under siege. That morning I drove Rachel to school and, as was my habit, hung out with cronies at the deli for breakfast. When I got up to leave, I noticed my feet were not responding. I nearly fell. My pals suggested I not drive, but I shrugged it off and drove anyway. I arrived at the set of *Sports Night* and headed directly for my dressing room. Putting on my wardrobe, I felt nauseated and fell off the couch. I couldn't get my left side to do a damn thing. They were calling my name over the PA, my scene was about to be shot, but I was helpless. The stage manager came looking for me. When he saw me on the floor, he rushed me to a nearby hospital. I told myself—and the doctor—this was just another TIA. When the doctor said, "You're having a stroke," I said, "You're crazy." Next morning, though, when he asked me to squeeze his hand, I couldn't.

Then I entered the dark tunnel. At the neurological recovery unit at UCLA for speech and physical therapy, I grew alarmed. I imagined the worst. I saw this as the single greatest catastrophe that could befall a thespian. My body would be crippled, and even worse, my speech, of which I was so proud, would be irreparably damaged. I would sound and look pathetic. Having pursued my craft and career with such fierce independence, I'd now be dependent on everyone for everything. My world would collapse around me. Donna would be repelled by my incapacitation and replace me with another man; Rachel would find me frightening and strange. In a bizarre twist, I'd become the real-life version of the Phantom of the Opera, a man whose deformity must be hidden from normal humans. I'd never be normal again. I'd go mad from frustration and fear. I'd sink into oblivion and die a miserable, lonely death.

And yet, as is often the case, the truth was not as dire as the scenario I feverishly imagined. While serious, the stroke never reached the level of extreme severity. The damage was far from total. My speech was only slightly affected. I retained a large measure of resonance and clarity. My singing voice was shot, a point of considerable pain given my vanity. But my mouth drooped only slightly. It would take determined effort to relearn basic skills. For months, movement would be difficult, but eventually—and remarkably soon—I would return to work. I would function. I would not go mad.

I soon saw that the most painful wound was to my pride. My gait was gone. A man's gait is his signature. And for a black man walking through the world of theater, gait is style. In the past, I'd been accused of fashioning an arrogant gait. I'd even been admonished to alter my walk and assume a more modest demeanor. I might have taken such advice to heart had I known what it meant to be obsequious, but the concept never registered with me. I thought back to that old adage "What is grace in a white man is arrogance in a black man." Now I suddenly saw my grace vanishing. I needed a cane as well as an adjustment in attitude. I hated the fact that rather than stride through life, I'd now limp; I'd have to struggle to get off the couch, fight to get out of the chair, exert enormous effort to move a few feet from bedroom to bathroom.

The tunnel was indeed dark. Depression hung over me, a gray cloud, inpenetrable, dense. My most precious commodity—freedom

—had been curtailed. I could no longer do what I wanted when I wanted to do it. I was diminished. At times I felt defeated.

And yet within this tunnel I saw shafts of light, rays of hope. Never in my life had I viewed myself as a victim. Why start now? Overcoming obstacles had long been my modus operandi. After several months of anguish, I started seeing the stroke as another in a long line of challenges. It would either take me down, or I could use it to build myself up. I chose the latter.

In so choosing, though, I couldn't ignore the stroke's permanent impact on my thinking. Mortality was no longer an abstract notion to be pondered before the fireplace. I could taste it. In the most visceral sense, I felt my time was limited. How much good time could I possibly have?

Five years? Ten? Fifteen? Everywhere I turned, I saw finiteness. My reaction was to cling to life. Life means work, and I was encouraged when Donna suggested to *Sports Night* producer Aaron Sorkin that Isaac Jaffe suffer a stroke as well, thus allowing me to continue the role. Sorkin agreed. I approached the "table reading," that part of the rehearsal process when the cast first goes through the script, with some anxiety. I was afraid I'd flub words, stumble over sentences, and appear inept. At times I did. But finally I found a rhythm that suited me—slower, to be sure, yet steady and reasonably dependable.

Work, though, was not enough. Neither was the rigorous, daily physical therapy—reciting scenes by Shakespeare to sharpen my diction, working out with weights, doing pull-ups and push-ups and upper-body exercises. Inevitably, the nights brought endless hours of rumination, when slipping back into the dark tunnel of gloom seemed frighteningly easy. During those times, Donna was wonderfully comforting. My fears of her walking out were unwarranted. She took my stroke in stride; she was attentive without being doting. She encouraged my exercise and, in a good way, kicked my ass. "You won't be satisfied," I kidded her, "until I'm running alongside your car with a wheelbarrow full of bricks." Her greatest aid, though, came in convincing Aaron Sorkin to write my stroke into the show.

It is not my nature to gush. I'm afraid that I never sufficiently expressed my gratitude to Aaron for continuing to pay me while I was unable to work. Aaron is the very definition of a mensch. When I—and Isaac Jaffee—returned to face the poststroke situations that challenged our professional lives, it was moving for everyone. The response was overwhelming. Fan letters poured in. Reviewers were generous with praise. I surely didn't see myself as a hero, merely as someone who chose to cling to life. When I agreed to present an Emmy that year, I did so knowing I'd limp out on stage and speak imperfectly. But I hoped that my imperfection might send a message to stroke sufferers: *We need not be ashamed; we need not concede.* The standing ovation indicated my message got across.

My return to *Sports Night*, while gratifying, proved fleeting. The show was cancelled after its second season. My disappointment was profound. I saw it as the one arena where my stroke was accepted. In the year after the cancellation, though, much of my strength returned. I auditioned and won several minor acting roles, voice-overs, and even one singing part for a cartoon. But when a major role came up for a film to be shot in Africa, the producer wanted to come to my home and see my physical condition for himself. He didn't put it that way, but I knew his motive. He came over; we chatted amiably for a half hour. The next day I was told he had decided not to cast me. My worst fear had come true. The stroke had cost me work.

Well, of course, the stroke would cost me work. How could it not? As crisp as my speech might now seem, as jaunty as my walk might appear, I still slurred and limped. I had to face facts. I absorbed many of the facts about strokes and served as spokesman for several organizations, going to conferences and making myself available for public service advertisements. I made an extra effort to reach out to the African Americans, who are at particularly high risk. I continue to cope as best as I can.

In these past few years, the stroke has given me ample opportunity to reflect. This memoir is an expression of those reflections. Because I was conservative during the days of my maximum earning power, I've been able to maintain a comfortable lifestyle. That's been a blessing. Another is the presence of my brother-in-law and dear friend, John Wesley, a talented actor who became a combination of executive assistant, confidante, and steady companion in the trying poststroke period.

"I first met Robert back in the eighties when I appeared on *Benson*," John recalled. "I'm academically trained, with a masters of fine arts in theater, and was a little tentative during the table reading. Robert noticed this and said, 'Look, you don't have to spook it up here. You don't have to apologize for being articulate and speaking well.' We became friends during that show and brothers-in-law in 1992 when I married Donna's sister Candy. After the stroke, I've tried to be his left hand. It's been a high honor to take this walk with him and witness his reaction to physical adversity. His sense of dignity never wavered; his patience is profound. In all sorts of circumstances, where others might have blown their cool, Robert never did. He stays steady. His great lesson to me as an actor—to all actors, and especially African American actors—is powerful: Never act out of fear. Act out of strength. Act out of self-knowledge and self-regard. If they reject you, fine. Let them find someone else. But don't personalize the rejection. Don't find fault with yourself. Walk through this perilous business with courage and class. Keep your head up. Respect yourself."

Crying has never been my style, but spontaneous crying is part of what they call the poststroke syndrome. It takes little to make me break out in tears. Oddly enough, I can control the impulse in a professional context—if I'm reading for a part or actually before the camera. But in a circle of friends or family, I might find myself weeping at unexpected moments. At first I was embarrassed. Now I accept it as the poststroke me. I'm more emotionally available than at any time in my life. I still struggle with my physicality. A few months back, I got my driver's license back. I wish I could do more. I still dream of dancing.

"I know Robert would still like to be dancing with me," said Donna. "We really didn't finish all our dancing, and I understand how that troubles him. I've accepted that, though, and don't sweat him about it."

Karma is absolute. You get what you give. The karmic irony of my life has much to do with women. I've known more than my fair share of good women—Marlene Williams, Karin Berg, and Faye Hauser among them. I believe they loved me with a purity and power I never understood. Certainly I never reciprocated. My faithlessness caused injury. The emotional damage was heavy. Not until I met Donna was I able to even consider my limitations in the area of love. She challenged my precepts and, to a large degree, caused me to reexamine my role in romantic relationships. I acted as though I was the only one who needed to be free. Donna taught me that freedom is a two-way street. I don't always like that reality, but I accept it.

I'm a slow learner. It has taken me most of my life to learn to love. I could receive love—from my grandmother, my sisters, my brother—but to actively give love was another matter. My ego got in the way. Ego forged by fear. The decimation of my ego was nothing I did on my own. Life did it for me. I'm proud of my hard-won successes, but now I'm also grateful for my failures. The failures helped crack my ego and grant me a degree of clarity, even a bit of humility. My heart aches when I think of the son I lost, but I rejoice when I think of the daughter who found me. I celebrate the accomplishments of my brilliant children—Pat, Kevin, Melissa, and Rachel—and cherish my relationships with my grandchildren and great-grandchildren.

Sometimes my children seek my advice. In the past, I gave it freely. I liked to hear myself sounding wise. These days I'm far more reticent. I speak less than at any time in my life, not because of my impairment but because I value silence more. I'm the guy who always had to have an opinion. It was inconceivable that I might step back from the fray. It has taken me seven decades to realize I don't have to know it all—or even know most of it. I can sit there, listen to others, nod appreciatively, and not say a word.

After a lifetime of living with the race issue, I feel obliged to conclude on a note of wisdom. I'm afraid I can't. As a child, I was blessed with a certain objectivity. I saw how whites were as frightened of us as we were of them. I also saw how fear, on both sides, turned to anger. I saw such anger as an impediment to my progress, and I avoided it. For these past seventy-three years, however, I can't say that the fear or anger, from blacks or whites, has diminished dramatically. To an alarming degree, fear and anger still abide. I deplore how racial prejudice in all forms continues to pervert our thinking; our public and private dialogues are polluted by misunderstanding and finger-pointing. Would that we could address one another as human beings, brother to brother, sister to sister, friend to friend, stranger to stranger. But history haunts us. That enormously evil act so central to our country's identity, the enslavement of blacks, still resonates with a ferocity that continues to confuse and embitter.

To assuage bitterness requires more than human effort. Relief comes from a source we cannot see but can only feel. I am content to call that source love. It remains a mystery. That mystery has many names in many religions, but, as far I can see, it cannot be understood; it must be absorbed. I am a man who has traveled from one segment of society to another. I was driven by fear; by selfishness; by financial need; by high-minded principles about being free. I was driven by the promise of a country that afforded success to those wily and tenacious enough to grasp and hold it. But now, as an old man, I can also see that I was driven by a force that sought a special kind of creativity. That creativity, for all its complexity, is nothing more or less than the expression of love.

# Filmography and Discography

## Actor

*The Adventures of Tom Thumb and Thumbelina* (2000) (V) . . . voice

*The Happy Prince* (1999) (TV) . . . Narrator

*The Lion King II: Simba's Pride* (1998) . . . voice of Rafiki

*Sports Night* (1998) (TV series) . . . Isaac Jaffe

*His Bodyguard* (1998) (TV movie) . . . Garrett
. . . aka *Silent Echoes* (1998) (TV)

*Merry Christmas, George Bailey* (1997) (TV) . . . Mr. Gower

*Crystal Cave* (1996) (TV) . . . Merlin
. . . aka *The Crystal Cave: Lessons from the Teachings of Merlin* (1996) (TV)

*Panic in the Skies!* (1996) (TV) . . . Rob Barnes

*Run for the Dream: The Gail Devers Story* (1996) (TV)
. . . Reverend Devers

*Pandora's Clock* (1996) (TV) . . . Ambassador Lee Lancaster
. . . aka *Doomsday Virus* (1997) (TV) (UK)

*First Kid* (1996) . . . Wilkes

*Spy Hard* (1996) . . . Agent Steve Bishop

*Happily Ever After: Fairy Tales for Every Child* (1995) (TV series)
. . . Narrator

*A Good Day to Die* (1995) (TV) . . . Mossburger
. . . aka *Children of the Dust* (1995) (TV)

*Cosmic Slop* (1994) (TV) . . . Gleason Golightly (segment "Space Traders")

*Greyhounds* (1994) (TV) . . . Robert Smith

*The Lion King* (1994) . . . voice of Rafiki

*The Meteor Man* (1993) . . . Mr. Reed

*Mastergate* (1992) (TV) . . . Sydney Sellers

*You Must Remember This* (1992) (TV) . . . Uncle Buddy

*Fish Police* (1992) (TV series) . . . voice of Detective Catfish

*Great American Celebration* (1991) (TV) . . . Himself

*Pacific Station* (1991) (TV series) . . . Det. Bob Ballard

*Death Warrant* (1990) . . . Hawkins

*Fire and Rain* (1989) (TV) . . . Carter

*The Robert Guillaume Show* (1989) (TV series) . . . Edward Sawyer

*The Penthouse* (1989/1) (TV) . . . Eugene St. Clair

*Lean on Me* (1989) . . . Dr. Frank Napier

*Christmas* (1988) (TV) . . . aka *John Grin's Christmas* (1988)

*They Still Call Me Bruce* (1987) . . . V. A. Officer Johnson

*Wanted: Dead or Alive* (1987) . . . Philmore Walker

*Perry Mason: The Case of the Scandalous Scoundrel* (1987) (TV)
. . . Harlan Wade

*North and South* (1985) (TV miniseries) . . . Frederick Douglass

*Prince Jack* (1984) . . . Martin Luther King

*The Kid with the 200 I.Q.* (1983) (TV) . . . Professor Mills

*The Kid with the Broken Halo* (1982) (TV) . . . Blake

*Seems Like Old Times* (1980) . . . Fred
. . . aka *Neil Simon's Seems Like Old Times* (1980)

*The Kid from Left Field* (1979) (TV) . . . Larry Cooper

*Benson* (1979) (TV series) . . . Benson DuBois (1979–1986)

*Soap* (1977) (TV series) . . . Benson (1977–1979)

*Good Times* (1974) (TV series) . . . Fishbone

*Superfly T.N.T.* (1973) . . . Jordan Gaines

## Producer

*Christmas* (1988) (TV)
. . . aka *John Grin's Christmas* (1988) (TV)

*The Kid with the 200 I.Q.* (1983) (TV) (executive)

## Director

*Christmas* (1988) (TV)
. . . aka *John Grin's Christmas* (1988) (TV)

## Notable TV Guest Appearances

*Moesha* (1996) . . . Arthur, Dee's Father in "All This and Turkey,
Too" (episode 6.10) 11/20/2000

*Touched by an Angel* (1994) . . . Judge Dawes in "Jones vs. God"
(episode 4.5) 10/19/1997

*Goode Behavior* (1996) . . . Dr. Baxter 2/1997

*Promised Land* (1996) . . . Martin Woolridge in "Christmas"
(episode 1.11) 12/17/1996

*Sparks* (1996) in episode: "Porky's Revenge" (episode 1.11) 11/18/1996

*The Fresh Prince of Bel-Air* (1990) . . . Mr. Fletcher in "You'd Better
Shop Around" (episode 4.18) 2/21/1994

*Burke's Law* (1994) in "Who Killed the Fashion King?" (episode 1.2)
1/14/1994

*Saved by the Bell: The College Years* (1993) . . . Dr. Arthur Hemmings in "A Question of Ethics" (episode 1.13) 12/21/1993

*Diagnosis Murder* (1993) . . . Father Morrissey in "Miracle Cure" (episode 1.1) 10/29/1993

*A Different World* (1987) . . . Professor Murphy in "Really Gross Anatomy" (episode 6.5) 10/22/1992

*L.A. Law* (1986) . . . Kenneth Rollins in "Diet, Diet My Darling" (episode 6.14) 2/27/1992

*A Different World* (1987) . . . Dean Winston in "Never Can Say Goodbye" (episode 4.24) 5/24/1991

*A Different World* (1987) . . . Dean Winston in "To Be Continued" (episode 4.25) 5/2/1991

*Good Times* (1974) . . . Fishbone in "Requiem for a Wino" (episode 5.11) 1977

*The Jeffersons* (1975) . . . Charles Thompson in "George Won't Talk" (episode 2.9) 11/8/1975

*All in the Family* (1971) . . . Dr. Franklin in "Chain Letter" (episode 6.3) 10/20/1975

*Sanford and Son* (1972) . . . Fred's lawyer in "Steinberg and Son" (episode 5.11) 10/1/1975

*Marcus Welby, M.D.* (1969) . . . Carothers in "The Soft Phrase of Peace" (episode 1.15) 1/6/1970

*Julia* (1968) in "Wheel Deal"


## Theater

*Cyrano* (1992)

*Phantom of the Opera* (1990)

*Guys and Dolls* (1976)

*Othello* (1973)

*Purlie* (1971)

*Jacques Brel Is Alive and Well and Living in Paris* (1968–1972)

*Ballad for Americans* (1965)

*Porgy and Bess* (1965–72)

*Golden Boy* (1965)

*Tambourines to Glory* (1963)

*Fly, Blackbird* (1962)

*Kwamina* (1961)

*Free and Easy* (1960)


## Recordings

*The Phantom of the Opera* (with Elizabeth Stack, 1998)

*This Is the Moment* (1994)

*As Times Goes By* (1993)

*The Pilgrims* (Columbia Records, 1964)

*Tambourines to Glory* (cast recording, 1963)

*Fly, Blackbird* (cast recording, 1962)

*Kwamina* (cast recording, 1961)

# Index

Page references to photos appear in italics.